A Guide to Mediation Training

An Insightful and Uncomplicated Guide to Learning Mediation

By

Stephen L. Sherwin

Dedications

This book is dedicated to those who would not otherwise have a voice for justice.

Acknowledgements

This book has been written to encourage personal accountability and restoration to human dignity.

Many thanks to Chris Cooper, my friend and colleague, who generously permitted me full use of his mediation training paradigm. He and I used this framework while training police officers across the state of Illinois.

This training manual incorporates material from *Mediation: Principles and Practice*, Third Edition by Kovach, Cooper's training module, my own practical experience, and various articles, books, and websites.

About the Author

Stephen Sherwin served in Vietnam with the United States Marine Corps. Upon being honorably discharged, he joined the Chicago Police Department as a police officer, during which time he supervised various units.

Stephen is certified in mediation, peace circle training, and anger management. He is a Stephen Ministry Leader and earned a doctoral degree in Adult and Higher Education. He is also a co-author of *AI and the Future of Law Enforcement*, published in May 2025.

Stephen currently serves as an assistant professor at Lewis University, where he teaches various criminal justice courses and mediation. He also hosts a podcast titled *At a Glance*, where he invites students, faculty, and other guests to discuss humanistic topics. The podcast airs on Spotify.

Foreword

I have been a part of the professional conflict resolution community for about 35 years. My journey began following my first active-duty stint as a United States Marine. While I was a young university student in New York City, I attended a college course registration event. The event was held in a gymnasium. Academic department advisors were stationed at tables to assist students in registering for classes, and the space was crowded with students like me, all looking for coveted class spots.

Upon learning that I needed three more credit hours, I tried to find a class with an opening. I was turned away from one table after another I was too late. The classes I sought were no longer available; they were filled. Discouraged and perhaps aimlessly meandering through the converted gym, I fortuitously came upon the table for what was then called the John Jay College of Criminal Justice Mediation Program.

I recall at least two people at the table. After 15 minutes of listening to an advisor's overview of mediation, I was persuaded to sign up for a mediation course. I am thankful for the sales pitch that day. I graduated from the John Jay program and thereafter utilized my mediation and conflict resolution skills as a police officer with the District of Columbia Police Department.

As a police officer patrolling some of D.C.'s most violent neighborhoods, my mediation and conflict resolution skills became very useful in my interactions with the citizens of the community. Later, as an academic, I joined Sherwin the author of this book and others in delivering mediation and conflict resolution training to thousands of people. The largest cohort we trained were police officers.

Through course instruction, Sherwin and I were able to show and, in some cases, convince countless police officers how they could enhance their productivity and effectiveness as law enforcement officers through the practice of good conflict resolution skills.

If your plan is to develop a skill set to practice as a mediator, then this book is for you. If you are an experienced mediator, this book is for you. *The Mediation Training Manual* presents the reader with a straightforward approach to understanding mediation practice through a robust conflict resolution lesson plan.

In this regard, I sense that for many readers of this book, the goal is to score home runs as a mediator to practice mediation as a polished, skilled conflict resolution professional. Whether you are a polished mediator or a student, we can agree that successful mediation practice means mastering the fundamental tenets of conflict resolution. *The Mediation Training Manual* enables such mastery.

In this regard, the book meticulously walks the reader through theories of why interpersonal conflicts occur, along with a robust focus on the laws that are implicated in a significant number of mediation events. And of course, *The Mediation Training Manual* enables the reader to embrace the mediator's toolbox, loaded with exceptional listening skills, word order presentation, and empathy, when possible, among many other skills.

Finally, *The Mediation Training Manual* conveys to the reader the significance of restorative justice processes.

Now, I hope I have convinced the reader to continue reading.

Christopher C. Cooper, JD, Ph.D.

Introduction

When you get to the top of the mountain, pull the next one up. Then there'll be two of you roped together at the waist, tired and proud, knowing the mountain, knowing the human force it took to bring both of you there. (Smith, n.d., cited by Eleveld, 2003, p. 128).

Smith's quote is from his poem *Pull the Next One Up*, which is an allegory that I juxtapose to the human journey that disputing parties experience in a mediation process. In the beginning of a conflict, the issues are like a molehill, where each party believes that only their positions and interests are relevant issues that can quickly be mitigated to their satisfaction. However, the molehill turns into a mountain of underlying issues that manifest unforeseen concerns and needs, which are often rooted in cultural differences, stigma, and lack of understanding.

The disputing parties soon realize that they need to work together, to trust and respect each other, to pull each other to the top of the mountain. The top of the mountain represents their agreement. In order to reach it, they need to trust the process, respect each other's perspectives, willingly compromise, and openly negotiate together.

There are three qualities needed to be a successful mediator. The first is to have presence or, as I prefer to say, heart. All the artful skills, methods, and processes will not be successful unless the mediator has presence. A mediator must be all in presence of mind and spirit.

The second quality is the concept of *not* utilizing logic. "The first realization for the psychologically informed mediator is that a perception shift will not be achieved through the application of logic or reason" (Randolph, 2016, p. 29). Where there is a conflict or dispute, it is often, if not always, predicated on emotion, not logic.

The third important quality for a mediator is to ensure that the disputants have a safe environment. "The invaluable benefit of building trust and creating rapport is that through this, the mediator can provide a safe environment in which the parties to the dispute can more openly and candidly express their views" (Randolph, 2016, pp. 35–36).

Mediation is infused with the values, skills, and methods that are needed for a restorative justice process. Mediation offers a sustainable solution for mitigating the fear, anger, and hate that polarize society. Let us work together from the spirit of our hearts, not from uncensored emotions.

The purpose for writing this mediation training manual was initially to assist me in teaching my mediation course. Then I realized its underlying universal utility. The training manual highlights the values, skills, and methods for creating a restorative justice process that empowers people to have a voice they would otherwise not have.

The manual provides the reader with orderly and simplistically concise, easy-to-follow steps for developing a sustainable mediation process. Throughout the manual, communication skills, laws, theories, and procedural steps are explained, providing mediators with essential methods to facilitate a meaningful mitigation process for obtaining a win-win reconciliation and agreement with parties experiencing conflicts or disputes.

I learned mediation and conflict resolution skills and methods that I have subsequently taught and trained others in for more than two decades. Prior to receiving formal mediation training, I unwittingly utilized mediation and conflict resolution skills. I was always intuitively proficient in successfully calming a situation or interpersonal dispute.

During my professional career as a street cop with the Chicago Police Department, I honed these skills. I realized early on in my police tenure that utilizing a humanitarian perspective to help citizens or de-escalate a police–citizen encounter garnered respect and trust among members of the community. It also made my working day less stressful, as I was able to successfully de-escalate situations without the use of force tactics.

I had the privilege of receiving my mediation training and certification from Christopher Cooper, J.D., Ph.D., with whom I subsequently worked to train law enforcement agencies throughout the state of Illinois in mediation and conflict resolution skills.

Cooper graciously permitted me to use carte blanche some of the material from our training seminars to write this book.

Under his leadership, I was part of a team of mediators providing mediation services to the Juvenile Division of the Cook County, Illinois, Circuit Court at the Markham Courthouse. We worked at the court for a year, during which I mediated many misdemeanor cases referred by a judge or assistant state's attorney. The experience of mediating court-referred disputes illuminated the overarching, ubiquitous utility of restorative justice changing lives.

Mediation empowers people to have a voice to negotiate, compromise, be accountable, and understand and respect differing perspectives. While mediating cases at the Juvenile Court, I witnessed not only a change in the lives of disputing parties in this case, youths but also the parents of young disputants.

In the beginning of the mediation sessions, it was normal for the parents to angrily profess their internalized rage, lack of trust in the mediation process, and contempt for the adverse party. I encountered parents of disputants enraged to the point of verbal abuse and threats of violence. Many times, it was the parents not the disputants with whom I had to enforce the ground rules established during the mediation orientation process.

However, after a few mediation sessions, I noticed the behavior and demeanor of the parents transform into understanding and acceptance. By the time an agreement was reached by all parties, the disputants and parents were genuinely happy, friendly, and satisfied with the mediation process. This experience made a profound impact on me, reinforcing the realization that mediation changes lives.

Mediation offers a second chance to preserve dignity and restore trust. As the youthful parties of a dispute observed their parents' transformation, they unwittingly experienced their own transformation and a second chance that forever changed their life course. The young disputants learned a better way to resolve disputes a way that keeps them out of courtrooms, maintains their dignity, and garners respect while preserving friendships.

Unfortunately, our society is replete with violence, hate, and a desire to punish. Too many of society's youth are without good social skills or the means to resolve issues peacefully. There is a societal outcry for justice, equality, tolerance for cultural diversity, and acceptance of personal orientations, but a lack of listening skills to understand and respect opposing perspectives.

However, mediation offers a process in which all voices are equal, respected, and empowered to speak. Mediation offers a process to listen to hear another perspective thus offering an opportunity to understand and forgive.

Mediation fosters personal transformation and acceptance of others' perspectives, values, interests, and positions without compromising individualism, but rather embracing inclusion. Mediation changes lives in a positive way.

My belief in the widespread usefulness of the mediation process was validated through a serendipitous encounter with a Native American, Spotted Eagle, a Sioux Indian lawyer and mediator. Spotted Eagle informed me that a Sioux burial ground in South Dakota had been destroyed by the Army Corps of Engineers while developing a waterway. The Sioux community petitioned the Federal Civil Court to hear their case against the Army Corps of Engineers for damage to their burial grounds.

Native Americans possess exceptional reverence for their burial grounds, as they are considered not only holy but highly sacred. The presiding federal court jurist referred the matter to Spotted Eagle for mediation. Although I did not mediate, I assisted as a consultant to Spotted Eagle. The mediation was a win-win for both parties. Although my role was limited, the experience was nonetheless remarkable. I not only benefited from the experience, but as a personal best, Spotted Eagle presented me with a copy of her published mediation book, which highlights a unique restorative justice process utilized by Native Americans.

Native Americans have employed mediation for centuries and continue to do so. Their use of mediation is multifaceted. The obvious purpose is to restore peace among members of their community who experience conflict. But the unique quality of their mediation process involves holding people accountable for their actions while elders conducting the mediation self-reflect on whether they, too, may have failed the person or people who caused harm to the community.

I have presented mediation lectures, discussions, and overviews in various venues such as George Mason University, Phoenix, Arizona, St. Paul, Minnesota, and local Chicago-area K–12 schools. I am witnessing a shift toward restorative justice practices such as mediation. This trend underscores the need for a concentrated effort to teach members of society the value of mediation by providing access to its training.

Although I am an optimist, I am also a realist. My optimism is that everyone receives training in the mediation process. My realism is the belief that at the very least, those with authority, leadership roles, and policymaking power should be trained in mediation so that they can establish mediation centers in their schools, businesses, and communities.

This, too, was and remains an undertaking I have been involved in. While working with Cooper to train various police departments, we trained the entire Orland Park, Illinois, police department along with several citizens of the Orland Park community. These citizens went on to establish a mediation center where residents could resolve interpersonal disputes.

In another effort to build mediation skills among youth, I and four of my students who had passed their mediation certification taught peer mediation to administrators, faculty, and students at Bolingbrook High School in Bolingbrook, Illinois. The mediation program remains a successful restorative justice initiative that fosters an inclusive culture of respect and trust, rather than relying on traditional disciplinary methods.

My goal in writing this book is to encourage the use of mediation as an alternative process for resolving conflicts through restorative justice. The criminal justice system is focused on punishment through a teleological lens. Mediation, by contrast, offers a process to improve community relations by addressing individual needs while promoting accountability when those needs are compromised due to a lack of respect, trust, or understanding of others' perspectives.

Mediation is a self-reflective process that helps improve interpersonal relationships a theme long understood and employed by Native Americans and other civilizations throughout history. The focus of mediation is personal growth, accountability, and the restoration of relationships not an eagerness to punish or cause harm.

Disputing parties decide their own outcomes and agreements by working together, healing through a process that preserves individual dignity, restores mutual respect and trust, and provides closure. The alternative is allowing a court to decide the fate of the disputing parties.

Chapter 1

Introduction to The Mediation Process

Mindfulness

"Mindfulness is the aware, balanced acceptance of the present experience. It is opening to or receiving the present moment, pleasant or unpleasant, just as it is, without either clinging to it or rejecting it" (Sockolov, 2018, p. 5).

"You are training the mind to be with one experience without distraction" (Sockolov, 2018, p. 3).

Sockolov (2018) offers these nine steps for a mindfulness experience:

Steps:

1. Sit in a comfortable position with your back erect, in a chair with both feet on the floor and hands resting on your thighs. Invite your audience to do the same.
2. Gently allow the eyes to close. Think of a theme color, place, or moment that brings thoughts of happiness, and ask your audience to do the same.
3. While focusing on one of these, guide your audience to do the same while encouraging them to relax their muscles and feel the natural rising and falling of their chest.
4. Gently instruct your audience to take a few deep breaths, breathing in through their nose and exhaling through their mouth, sensing the feeling of doing this while continuing to focus on a color, place, or moment of happiness in their lives.
5. Continue to softly instruct the audience to breathe through their nose and exhale through their mouth. Gently encourage the audience to allow the thing they are thinking of to fully enter their mind to feel the moment, feel the love.
6. Allow for a few quiet moments for the audience to concentrate.
7. Gently instruct the audience to open their eyes.
8. After everyone is back in the moment, begin by sharing your experience. Upon conclusion, invite members from the audience to share theirs.

9. Conclude with a salutation (pp. 3–4).

Why mindfulness? How does it help a mediator mediate?

The answer is simple. I remember my first time testifying in court for an arrest I made. I was filled with angst I had someone's life at stake. I remembered reading something about breathing exercises to calm a person: take a deep breath and count to ten. It worked to a degree. Then I was exposed to meditation that worked better. I used that method every time I had to testify, which was so many times I lost count. Nonetheless, each time I felt anxious, I utilized a meditation exercise to give me relief.

I subsequently used meditation as a mediator it worked there too.

How does that fit into mediation? Twofold.

First, in each mediation session, a mediator will experience angst. Mindfulness helps the mediator find self-calm prior to working with the parties in a dispute.

Second, the practice of mindfulness provides a mediator with a calm presence that radiates an atmosphere of respect, trust, and care. This, in turn, relieves the angst and trepidation the parties feel about their expectations of the mediation process, thereby providing a safe environment.

Community Agreement

The assumption is that mediation will be taught or trained to a group of individuals who might not share a personal or professional acquaintance. Nonetheless, as a group of trainees, we form both a community and a culture. As participants in a training group, we need to develop a community and culture that foster respect, comfort, openness, curiosity, and care.

Community agreements help us accomplish these values by working together to relate in confident, sustainable ways, designing a spirit of community and a consensually accepted culture. Utilizing these methods and tools challenges everyone to recognize, appreciate, and understand individual differences, providing a transformative learning experience. Community agreements offer a template for developing ground rules, equality, empowerment, and confidentiality during the mediation process.

Types of Disputes

- **Interpersonal Dispute:** A disagreement between two individuals involving significant resentment and discontent.
    - *Rule:* Interpersonal disputes are normal, healthy, and in some cases, productive. Disputes enable us to take note of a problem.
- **Intrapersonal Dispute:** A conflict that occurs solely in a person's own mind.
- **Unresolved (Episodic) Dispute:** Occurring occasionally and at irregular intervals.

Introduction to Mediation

Mediation is the intervention of a neutral third party **you**, the third-party intervenor (TPI) who provides a formal process for disputing parties to negotiate a successful reconciliation.

The term *mediation* can be defined as:

A neutral third party assisting disputants in resolving a conflict or dispute. Specifically, the neutral third party (the mediator) is an active and assertive facilitator in the dispute resolution process. The mediator does not impose a decision. Rather, they assist the disputants in creating their own agreement.

The third party sets the stage for mediation by listening to the disputants, helping them frame the issues, and keeping the mediation process goal-directed so that the parties can develop their own resolution.

The mediation process is a **win-win** process. When the dispute has been resolved, the parties walk away with a resolution but not with exactly what each party originally wanted. Instead, the parties compromise. In mediation, a compromise is considered a win-win resolution because the disputants decided on the nature of the compromise themselves. Since it was their decision, each party walks away from the dispute resolution process as a winner. Usually, the process through which parties reach a compromise is a collective one they work together to create it.

A neutral third-party (mediator):

- Assists disputants in resolving a conflict or dispute
- Does not impose a decision
- Listens to the disputants
- Helps identify issues
- Keeps the mediation process goal-directed so the disputants can create their own resolution

Brief History of Mediation

Mediation is based on a restorative justice paradigm for resolving interpersonal disputes, such as conflicts between friends, coworkers, or adversaries. The method involves a third party intervening in an interpersonal dispute and assisting the disputants in resolving the matter. In mediation, the mediator never imposes a resolution; instead, the mediator supports the disputing individuals in creating their own solution.

The mediation method is not new. Although it may appear to be new to some in the Western world, it has only recently gained popularity there.

In China, "the People's Republic of China has been actively practicing mediation to resolve conflicts and agreements since ancient times" (Yuliia, 2020, p. 2455). The Chinese utilize mediation as a platform for moral and ethical norms, as well as a lawful means for regulating social relationships (Kovak, 2013, as cited by Yuliia, 2020).

The Mennonites and Quakers are among religious groups that have used mediation for centuries and continue to use it today. These groups practice mediation for interpersonal disputes within their respective communities. In times when ecclesiastical law was prominent, mediation constituted a core component of the justice system (Kriesberg, 2009).

Native American cultures, such as Indigenous Indian tribes, utilize a mediation process through a peace circle methodology. They form a circle of elders who listen to interpersonal disputes or address violations of tribal laws or rules that have harmed the broader community. The entire community is invited to observe the mediation process conducted by the elders (Spotted Eagle, 2000).

Mediation is an alternative dispute resolution method. It is considered "alternative" and unconventional because, although it is growing in popularity, it is not yet used routinely. Therefore, mediation fits into the category of Alternative Dispute Resolution (ADR).

In 1980, the U.S. Congress passed the Dispute Resolution Act, which called for the establishment of ADR programs across the country. This act encouraged the use of mediation. Nineteen years later, the Dispute Resolution Act of 1998 further expanded ADR's reach. The 1998 act requires federal agencies to use ADR methods such as mediation whenever possible, rather than relying solely on traditional legal methods like litigation. The federal government recognized that mediation is not only a cost-effective way to handle civil cases, but it also aligns with restorative justice principles that promote lasting, peaceful resolutions and closure. Other countries have passed similar legislation (Kriesberg, 2009).

Today, mediation is used worldwide to address a variety of disputes, including neighbor disagreements, employment issues, marital disputes, and landlord-tenant conflicts. Trained mediators facilitate a process that enables disputants to negotiate their own resolutions, avoiding costly court proceedings and promoting win-win outcomes.

Mediation skills offer an effective method for addressing and resolving the conflicts that naturally arise from social interactions and encounters. The list of people who can benefit from mediation training is virtually unlimited and includes lawyers, police officers, teenagers, human resource professionals, and K–12 schoolteachers, to name just a few.

Mediation can be used to handle a variety of interpersonal disputes. Examples include:

A. Landlord–tenant disputes

B. Domestic situations not involving violence

C. Distribution of assets (e.g., divorce, dissolved business partnerships)

D. Neighbor disputes

E. Customer–merchant disputes (e.g., small claims court-type cases)

F. Accession

G. Labor–management disputes

Chapter 2

Distinguishing Between Conflict and Dispute

Conflict

Conflict is defined as:

"An encounter with arms, a fight, a battle, a prolonged struggle" (Kovach, 2004, p. 2). For this course, conflict is defined "as a set of divergent aims, methods, or behavior; an expressed struggle between at least two interdependent parties who perceive incompatible goals, scarce rewards, and interference from the other party in achieving their goals" (Kovach, 2004, p. 2).

- A clash of interests
- Personal, racial, class, caste, political, and international issues
- Differences of opinion and disagreements between people
- Builds up to a conflict resolution stage that provides a return to routine interaction
- Conflict is a natural and very common phenomenon in relationships among people

- Conflicts at every level have some common characteristics and dynamics
- People get involved in conflicts because their interests or their values are challenged, or because they perceive that their needs have not been met

Conflict usually is manifest conflict—conflict that we can readily observe. Yet in many situations, even where there is such overt conduct, underlying conflict also exists.

Although the terms "dispute" and "conflict" have distinct definitions, they are used interchangeably in the field of dispute resolution.

Dispute

1. To engage in an argument or debate
2. To question
3. To contest
4. To oppose
5. To have a controversy or difference of opinion
6. To quarrel

Disputes sometimes have two layers. The bottom layer is defined as the latent dispute (or underlying dispute), and the top layer is defined as the manifest dispute.

Illustrated below is a volcano erupting. The eruption itself is the manifest dispute, but hidden underneath (the bottom layer), rumbling inside the volcano, is the latent dispute (underlying dispute) which is often the real reason for the conflict.

The Top Layer, the Lava Erupting, is the Manifest Dispute: Erupting as Anger and Blame

The bottom layer of the volcano is the latent dispute (underlying issues):

Misunderstandings

Embarrassment

Fear

Envy

Guilt

Resentment

Anxiety

Insecurity

Feeling overwhelmed

Worry

Rage

Exhaustion

Moodiness

Perception

Perception:

- The ability to see, hear, or become aware of something through the senses
- The state of being or process of becoming aware of something through the senses

- A way of regarding, understanding, or interpreting something; a mental impression
- Intuitive understanding and insight

People can look at the same object or be confronted by the same issue at the same time and see, hear, or identify them differently. Each person perceives things through their own value processes. This does not necessarily make them wrong or right—merely that they have a different perspective.

Randolph (2016) argues that "Perceptions are assumptions that we all make—about the people we meet, their appearance, their intellect, their behavior, and, most importantly in disputes, their motivations" (p. 104).

"The single most vital objective of a mediator is to secure an attitude shift on the part of one or more of the parties in the conflict. The shift of attitude will be fundamentally one of perception. The perceptions may be intrapersonal, involving a change in the party's own self-awareness and self-concept. The mediator thus seeks gently to nudge the parties to move to a different perception—of themselves, of each other and of the dispute" (Randolph, 2016, p. 28).

The best part of having different perceptions is when someone with a different perception understands an opposing one.

Chapter 3

Legal Issues and Theories

Mediation is frequently referred by the courts as a method to mitigate misdemeanor and civil cases. Thus, it is important to understand some legal terms used by the criminal justice system.

Criminal Law

A system of law concerned with the punishment of those who commit crimes. Contrasted with civil law.

Criminal Court

A court of law in which criminal cases are tried and determined.

Prosecutor

A lawyer who conducts the case against a defendant in a criminal court. Also called a prosecuting attorney.

Criminal Defendant

A criminal defendant is the accused in a criminal action. A criminal defendant usually defends or denies the relief or recovery sought in an action or suit. A criminal defendant has the right to take the witness stand and to testify in their own defense.

Civil Law

The system of law concerned with private relations between members of a community rather than criminal, military, or religious affairs. Contrasted with criminal law.

COA (Court of Appeals)

A court to which appeals are taken in a federal circuit or a state.

Plaintiff

A person who brings a case against another in a court of law. Compare with defendant. (In a criminal case, neither the prosecutor nor the victim is identified as the plaintiff.)

Civil Case Defendant

A civil defendant is a person who has been accused by another party of a civil wrong. The person bringing the lawsuit against the defendant is known as the "plaintiff." In civil cases, both the plaintiff and the defendant appear in court, though arrests in civil suits are rare.

Civil Court

A court dealing with noncriminal cases.

Injunction

A judicial order that restrains a person from beginning or continuing an action threatening or invading the legal rights of another, or that compels a person to carry out a certain act, for example, to make restitution to an injured party.

Administrative Rule

Administrative rules are officially promulgated agency regulations that have the force and effect of law. Generally, these rules elaborate the requirements of a law or policy. Each state has its own set of administrative rules, which are passed by the state legislature.

Affidavit

A written statement confirmed by oath or affirmation, for use as evidence in court.

SOL (Statute of Limitations)

Refers to the maximum time frame in which a party can pursue a particular legal matter, criminal or civil. Generally, when the statute of limitations is tolled (delayed or held off), the maximum time frame is extended.

Prima Facie

Based on the first impression; accepted as correct until proved otherwise.

Liability

The state of being responsible for something, especially by law.

A thing for which someone is responsible, especially a debt or financial obligation.

A person or thing whose presence or behavior is likely to cause embarrassment or put one at a disadvantage.

Motion

In the context of law, a motion means a request or application made to a court or jury by a plaintiff or litigant in connection with a case for a judgment or order. In parliamentary law, a motion refers to the formal mode in which a member submits a proposed plan or measure for the approval of the parliamentary meeting.

Ex Parte

Done with respect to or in the interests of one side only or of an interested outside party. "On behalf of or involving only one party to a legal matter and in the absence of, and usually without notice to, the other party." An ex parte motion refers to relief granted in such a manner. Used in citations to indicate the party seeking judicial relief in a case (e.g., Ex Parte Jones, 7 U.S. 2, 1866).

Pro Se

Derived from the Latin term that means "for oneself." This process can occur in any court proceeding where the party acting in pro se legal representation is the plaintiff or the defendant, or if the person is representing themself in a civil or criminal case.

Promissory Note

A written promise to pay a debt. An unconditional promise to pay on demand, or at a fixed or determined future time, a particular sum of money to, or to the order of, a specified person or to the bearer.

Restraining Order

A legally binding order of the court, enforceable by law enforcement officials as well as the court. Such protective orders are issued not only to protect victims from violence but also from other forms of abuse, nuisance, and stalking.

Discovery

A fact-finding process that takes place after a lawsuit has been filed and before trial in the matter, to allow the parties in the case to prepare for settlement or trial.

Assets

An asset is anything with a monetary value attached. Assets may be real or personal property, which may be used for payment of debts.

A tangible asset is one whose value depends on particular physical properties. These include reproducible assets such as buildings or machinery and non-reproducible assets such as land, a mine, or a work of art.

An intangible asset is one that has no physical being, other than writing, to make evident its existence. For example, the goodwill of a business and a promissory note evidencing a debt are intangible assets.

Cross Complaint

1. A claim brought by a defendant against another party to the lawsuit.

2. A claim brought by a defendant against a person not a party to the original lawsuit for a related cause of action.

Felony

A crime, typically one involving violence, regarded as more serious than a misdemeanor, and usually punishable by imprisonment for more than one year or by death.

Misdemeanor

A crime that carries a less severe punishment than a felony. Specifically, a crime punishable by a fine and by a term of imprisonment not to be served in a penitentiary and not to exceed one year.

Violation

A violation of law is any act (or, less commonly, failure to act) that fails to abide by existing law. Violations generally include both crimes and civil wrongs. Some acts, such as fraud, can violate both civil and criminal laws.

Plea Bargain

Plea bargains are agreements between defendants and prosecutors in which defendants agree to plead guilty to some or all the charges against them in exchange for concessions from the prosecutors.

Covenant

A covenant is a restrictive clause regarding real estate that governs its use. For example, the requirement that the premises be used solely for residential purposes. Covenants are restrictive requirements found in deeds and other documents pertaining to real estate.

Title

Title is the sum total of legally recognized rights to the possession and ownership of property. It is the union of all elements—such as ownership, possession, and custody—constituting the legal right to control and dispose of property.

Contract

An agreement between private parties creating mutual obligations enforceable by law. The legal contract age varies depending on each state. A contract is one of the oldest laws around and is an agreement that is legally enforceable between at least two parties. The parties in the contract need to be mentally competent adults, which often means they cannot be minors.

Juvenile Delinquent

A person who is underage (usually below 18), who is found to have committed a crime in states which have declared by law that a minor lacks responsibility and thus may not be sentenced as an adult.

Dispute Resolution Approaches

A third party is sometimes needed to help people (disputants) resolve their interpersonal disputes. The third-party intervener (TPI) is neutral, that is, they remain objective. The TPI must not play favorites; they must remain in the middle, equally detached from each disputant.

Significant dispute resolution approaches include:

1. **Arbitration**: The TPI makes the decision that is based on facts, not on preference.
2. **Adjudication**: This is arbitration but in a court of law. Adjudicators (judges or hearing officers) impose decisions in adjudicatory settings.
3. **Mediation**: The TPI does not impose a decision but helps the disputants fashion their own resolution.
4. **Facilitation**: A process that involves a TPI simply doing things to get the disputants to communicate.
5. **Negotiation**: A process by which the disputants work without a third party to resolve a dispute. Granted, in mediation there is a great deal of negotiating, but the mediation process is not called negotiation.

Theories Underlying Interpersonal Conflict

The mediation process is predicated on sociological theories that provide the mediator with insights into manifestations that cause a variety of human behaviors. It is important for the mediator to acquire knowledge of these theories to recognize when they are exhibited by disputants. This helps the mediator identify underlying issues and thereby ensure impartiality, respect, and justice during the mediation process.

Anomie

Émile Durkheim (1858–1917) developed his theory of anomie based on his view that "crime is an essential part of society and a function of its internal conflict." Durkheim defines anomie as "the absence or weakness of rules and social norms in any person or group; without these rules or norms, an individual may lose the ability to distinguish between right and wrong" (Siegel and Worrall, 2021, pp. 99–100). Durkheim classified this phenomenon as a sense of "normlessness." Without understanding the rules and norms of society, and thereby not being held accountable for independent actions or responsible for variations in perception, conflict arises.

Understanding anomie provides the mediator with empathetic insight into why or how a conflict can manifest into a dispute. The following are some examples:

- Accession
- Public places
- Cultural

There are other manifold reasons for the application of anomie to mediation. Disputants might lack the skills to mitigate a dispute on their own. They may not know what mediation is. They may feel that no one cares about them or whether they are allowed to have a voice to lawfully defend their perspectives. Therefore, it is of great importance that a mediator possesses the ability to explain the values of mediation to the disputants. Doing so will help build trust among the disputants, ensure a successful reconciliation, and lead to an equitable agreement.

Cultural Conflict Theory

Hass, Moloney, and Chambliss (2017) cite Thorsten Sellin, a sociologist who developed the cultural conflict theory while conducting research on the causes of criminality. Sellin argued that the "root cause" of committing crimes was based on variations in values regarding what constitutes acceptable or unacceptable behavior. These variations were a result of cultural diversity, which "produces a clash in values because different people are socialized in different ways. Thus, conduct norms, those rules of acceptable behavior we learn early on in life, will vary" (Hass et al., 2017, p. 399). Understanding cultural diversity is an important requisite for mediators.

Mediators will often encounter disputants whose conflict issues stem from a clash in values resulting from variations in cultural norms about what is acceptable or unacceptable behavior. Understanding cultural conflict can help the mediator assess whether the "primary conflict" (Vito and Maahs, 2017, p. 178) among disputants is the result of a variation in cultural norms. It also helps the mediator quantify legitimacy, equality, and respect to stimulate trust in the mediation process.

Culture conflict theory also presumes that people outside the mainstream may adapt to subcultures, which have their own norms and values and may celebrate criminal or deviant behavior.

(Schmalleger, p. 275)

Dramaturgy

Goffman (1959) introduced the theory of dramaturgy, which is based on research studying how people communicate. The study concluded that people assume roles like actors on an imaginary stage and intentionally calculate performances designed for specific audiences. As the audience varies in purpose and expectations, so does the actor's performance. Dramaturgy suggests that a person's identity constantly changes as situations and people change during interactions.

Once the actor has completed their performance, Goffman (1959) proposed that they retreat to an area where they perform in a manner that is not visible or audible to an audience. He categorizes these areas as follows:

Front Stage

This is when an actor consciously and deliberately performs a part designed for a specific audience. For example, a server in a restaurant performs with polite dignity toward customers. The server reads their audience and delivers a performance to please and gratify in a way that solicits financial compensation in return.

Back Stage

This is when an actor retreats from the front stage to an area away from the audience. Backstage provides the actor an opportunity to relax from their role and engage in a more casual, less controlled method of communication. For example, the server retreats to the kitchen, out of sight and hearing of customers, and may behave in ways that would be inappropriate in front of them.

Off Stage

This is when an actor is no longer performing for an audience and returns to their identity and unfiltered self-expression, beliefs, and opinions. They are unaware of being observed and are in a relaxed state of anonymity. A person off stage may do or say things they would never intentionally do in front of an audience.

Social Exchange Theory

"Social exchange occurs within structures of mutual dependence, in which actors are dependent on each other for valued outcomes" (Molm, Takahashi, and Peterson, 2000, p. 1398). These dependent outcomes are essential for developing trust between disputants in mediation. Trust in the process and in the belief that both parties will have equal power and opportunity to negotiate a balanced outcome is key. "Inequalities in power and dependence create power-imbalanced relations" (Molm et al., 2000, p. 1399). A power imbalance can lead to unscrupulous behavior, diminishing the value of mediation and eroding trust and respect for the process and all involved.

Trust and respect galvanize the disputants' confidence to enter into a negotiation where risks and rewards are carefully weighed.

Basic Points in Exchange Theory

1. The gratification experienced in many social settings is contingent on the actions of others.
2. A great deal of human suffering, as well as much of human happiness, has its source in the actions of others.

Two Types of Rewards That People Give Each Other

1. **Extrinsic**: Tangible rewards (e.g., money)
2. **Intrinsic**: Intangible rewards (e.g., love, respect)

Social Attraction

A person or institution that offers rewards to individuals is highly attractive socially. Social attraction explains when and why the rewards are given. The main force that draws and ties people together is social attraction.

Social Exchange Theory gives the TPI (third-party intervener) theories as to why people are involved in a battle, or why the disputants are in mediation. Most importantly, this theory helps the TPI recognize the latent dispute or the underlying conflict. If the TPI understands the dispute resolution perspective in Exchange Theory, they will have an easier time spotting interests and, therefore, be able to distinguish between the manifest dispute and the latent (or underlying) dispute.

Exchange Theory is like the boiling lava of a volcano (depicted earlier in the illustration of an erupting volcano). Thus, the Exchange Theory lava is understood by someone who knows how to examine it. The TPI needs to always look for boiling lava. In it, the TPI is likely to find the underlying causes of the manifest dispute. The cause is more easily understood if the TPI has knowledge of Exchange Theory and how problematic exchanges lead to interpersonal conflict.

At the lowest level, Exchange Theory is about tangible and intangible things that we exchange in society. Specifically:

- How these exchanges lead to interpersonal conflicts
- When these exchanges lead to interpersonal conflicts
- Why these exchanges lead to interpersonal conflicts
- The amount and quality of an exchange that leads to interpersonal conflicts

The following are some of the exchanges (issues) in an interpersonal relationship that lead to interpersonal conflict:

- A power imbalance in the relationship – one party dominates too much. In a mediation, when the TPI notices a power imbalance in a negotiation, there needs to be intervention.
- Social attraction is too low. The cause of the conflict or dispute may have something to do with:
    - The other person is no longer being perceived as socially attractive.
    - The other person is no longer perceived as being able to provide the rewards the first party wants or has

chosen not to provide them. (Essentially, this is the problem of inadequate social rewards.)

  - Rewards serve to strengthen social ties.
  - Inadequate rewards lead to a deterioration of social ties.

- There is unequal reciprocity. One party is not giving enough (of extrinsic or intrinsic rewards), or a party is not pulling their weight.
- Negative behavior is reinforced via rewards. For example, a person may behave the way they do because of the minimal reward they receive for the behavior. How can the behavior be stopped? Will the disputant forgo receiving the reward?

The way the TPI is perceived by the disputants—and how the TPI perceives them—is an important issue in keeping the mediation goal-oriented. The TPI must continuously be aware of physical and verbal signals while interacting with disputants, as a lack of these may cause negative perceptions that could lead to discomfort, distrust, and a lack of care for the needs of a disputant. These signals are outlined in the following paragraphs.

Empathy

"Empathy is looking at the world from someone else's perspective to experience what the person is feeling—and then expressing your understanding of those feelings to that person" (Bretscher and Haugk, 2023, p. 15).

Importance of Empathy

The ability to empathize with another person or demonstrate empathy is one of the most valuable abilities for mediators. Empathy is not, and should not be mistaken for, sympathy (Kovach, 2004, p. 65).

A significant aspect of the mediation process is to provide disputants an opportunity to vent—to express their feelings without being judged, criticized, or repressed from acknowledging their perspectives or feelings of being emotionally hurt, disrespected, or misunderstood. "People who are struggling often feel misunderstood, since others may minimize or dismiss the feelings they express" (Bretscher and Haugk, 2023, p. 25).

Thus, enabling disputants to have a voice where they would otherwise not have one (as in a court) provides them with emotional relief and a realization that their perspective and feelings matter. Disputants who are empowered through an empathetic lens illuminate their interests, thus "they can be motivated by concerns for others in addition to their own interests" (Paternoster, Jaynes, and Wilson, 2017, p. 851).

Empathy requires effective listening—an important factor for the mediator's focus on issue spotting and identifying underlying concerns related to self-interest to help keep the process goal-oriented.

Symbolic Interaction

"People communicate through gestures, signs, words, and images that stand for, or represent, other things (symbols)" (Vito and Maahs, 2017, p. 159). These symbols are important because they help a mediator recognize and interpret behavior and reactions that reveal underlying issues.

People often use symbolism to create an image—whether good or bad, false or true—or to cloak their true self. Wearing clothing, jewelry, body art, or smoking a cigarette provides symbols that "help people understand and define themselves" (Vito and Maahs, 2017, p. 160).

"The looking glass self" galvanizes self-reflection in how a person defines themselves based on how others perceive them. In other words, when a person believes that others see them portraying a certain role or character through their image, they will act out that role or character.

There are two caveats to symbolic interactionism:

1. The way people see others can cause a stigma or labeling of that person, thus manifesting a bias.
2. The mediator needs to reflect on their own symbolic interactionism to avoid portraying symbols that could be interpreted as biased, judgmental, or critical.

Empowerment

The mediator empowers the disputants.

The mediator is an active, assertive facilitator but does not impose a decision. The mediator assists the disputants in fashioning their own agreement.

The psychological effect of empowerment:

1. Creates motivation to solve the problem.
2. Provides stability of the resolution.

Empowerment is an important element in the mediation process. It encourages disputant confidence in possessing an equal voice in the negotiation process. Empowerment instills confidence in the disputants regarding their right to have a voice, equally and without bias, to profess their perspectives while negotiating a favorable agreement.

Chapter 4
Mediation Skills

Listening

Do you hear — or do you hear?

"The most powerful skills that can be deployed by a listener to ensure that the speaker feels truly heard are those of reflecting back, paraphrasing, and summarizing" (Randolph, 2016, pp. 39–40).

Listening to the needs of others requires working from the heart and having wholesight, thus enabling empathy. Remember that empathy means offering understanding without necessarily condoning words or actions.

Active listening is a method that develops trust between the mediator and the disputants. It enables the mediator "to understand their perceptions, feel their emotions, and hear what they are trying to say" (Fisher and Ury, 1983, p. 35). Active listening demonstrates to the disputants that the mediator is paying attention and cares.

Another Listening Skill

Active listening is also known as reflective listening. It is a skill used for paraphrasing and reflecting back to the disputant what they said. Reflective listening provides the mediator an opportunity to clarify, confirm, or reword their understanding of an issue (Kreidler, 1984).

Reflective listening is a communication method involving two principal steps:

- To understand a speaker's idea
- To offer the idea back to the speaker to confirm that it was understood correctly

Example: The mediator states, "What I think I hear you saying is…" It is important to understand the **needs** of the disputants.

Good communication is a process that involves both the sending and the receiving of messages. Therefore, the most important function of the mediator's role is to be a good listener.

When the mediation process begins, the mediator's chief focus should be on employing direct interpersonal, or face-to-face, communication. The mediator must remain aware of the continuous interchange of messaging throughout the process.

Communication takes place in four forms:

Verbal: Interpersonal communication can take several forms. The Oxford Dictionary defines them as:

1. **Two-way conversation:** A conversation between two people in which both parties exchange information. The four main components of the two-way communication model are:
    - Sender
    - Receiver
    - Message
    - Response
2. **Listening (primarily one-way communication):** Used to urge someone to pay attention to what is being said.
3. **Sender:** A person who sends or transmits a message.
4. **Interactive:** Two people influencing or having an effect on each other.

Disputes often exist when two people fail to communicate with each other or communicate imprecisely. Cultural differences can be a cause of miscommunication. When cultural differences compromise effective communication, the mediator should seek reliable methods of communication or involve an interpreter to assist the parties during the mediation process.

Listen for the Disputants' Needs

"If we had a clear statement of each person's needs—what those parties need right now from each other—we will then discover what can be done to get everybody's needs met. These become the strategies the parties agree to implement after the mediation session concludes and the parties leave the room" (Rosenberg, 2015, p. 164).

Other communication issues that might impede the mediation process—and that a mediator needs to be acutely aware of—include expressions such as *ah*, *um*, *you know*, or long pauses. These can lessen the impact of a statement and polarize the individuals. The intentional use of sarcasm, undesirable jokes, or derisive questioning can also inhibit effective communication.

A disputant may try to avoid acknowledging the other party's concerns by muting them. Kovach offers five basic methods individuals use to silence another:

1. Interrupting
2. Changing the topic
3. Avoiding the topic
4. Blaming internal procedures
5. Sidetracking

(p. 54)

Rosenberg (2015) offers:

"The hearing that is only in the ears is one thing. The hearing of the understanding is another. But the hearing of the spirit is not limited to any one faculty, to the ear, or to the mind. Hence it demands the emptiness of all the faculties. And when the faculties are empty, then the whole being listens. There is then a direct grasp

of what is right there before you that can never be heard with the ear or understood with the mind" (p. 91).

1. **Issue Spotting:**

   This is the process of identifying key issues and underlying issues. By being a good listener, the mediator is able to spot the relevant issues. Remember the difference between a manifest dispute and a latent dispute. In many cases, the mediator must be proactive in identifying the underlying issues. These are the things that the disputing parties are not talking or arguing about—but should be, in most situations.

These issues are often predicated on two important concepts: needs (positions) and interests. Picard (1998) states, "The real problem in conflict situations is not the position (what they want) of each person, but the reasons underlying the position (feelings, needs, fears, concerns). These are interests and they are what motivate us. A position is adopted on the basis of interests" (p. 95).

Position: A person's point of view or attitude toward something.

Interest: A stake, share, or involvement in an undertaking, especially a financial one.

Methods Mediators Can Use to Discover Underlying Interests:

- Ask why, why not, or what
- Use a less direct approach that involves the mediator listening carefully and being aware of subtleties
- Use reflective listening
- Be cognizant of the needs and interests of the participants

2. **Articulate Issues:**

   To articulate an issue is to express it clearly and clarify it. The mediator efficiently neutralizes, rephrases, and paraphrases what the disputants have said.

Early in the mediation process, each disputant has a chance to tell the mediator why they are upset. In step three of the mediation process, it is necessary for the mediator to repeat back to the disputants what was heard from them about why they are upset. The mediator does this to help the disputants frame the issues and to make sure that everyone, including the mediator, fully understands what is going on.

To do this effectively, the mediator neutralizes, rephrases, and paraphrases what the disputants have said. It is sometimes all about using euphemisms. So, when the disputant says about the other disputant, "He is a very strange guy," the mediator may say, "What I think I hear you saying is, he is different from other people whom you know."

Rosenberg (2015) suggests that our paraphrasing take the form of questions that reveal our understanding while eliciting any necessary corrections from the speaker. Questions may focus on these components:

- What others are observing: "Are you reacting to how many evenings I was gone last week?"
- How others are feeling and the needs generating their feelings: "Are you feeling hurt because you would have liked more appreciation of your efforts than you received?"
- What others are requesting: "Are you wanting me to tell you my reasons for saying what I did?" (p. 96)

Identify, Reframe, and Restate: The Use of Language

As the parties describe the dispute or conflict, the mediator begins to identify the primary issues of contention. The way these issues are described is how they are framed. The mediator may then restate the issue and reframe the problem.

"Reframing involves changing the wording, concept, or description of a piece of information to make it easier to understand or accept" (Slaikeu, 1996, p. 231).

For example:

- Disputant's Original Comment: "He is a moronic scumbag."
- Mediator Reframes the Comment: "What I hear you saying is that he lacks the ability to be pleasant."

As a mediator, restating what a party has said and reframing the way a party has related a problem are two of the most effective tools used to move parties away from inflexible positions. There are two techniques that mediators may utilize to successfully achieve this:

- **Restate:** Paraphrasing a few sentences in a way that reflects what the speaker said, but with a slight change of focus or by removing offensive language.
- **Reframe:** A reflective statement about the problem or issues, used to help the parties view the problem or concern in a different light.

By using more neutral language, the mediator urges the parties to approach the dispute in a more positive manner. This technique is often effective in de-polarizing the parties. Restatements may be used by the mediator several times during the process.

The mediator must focus on uncovering or discovering the underlying or influential interests of the parties. This is the mediator's most fundamental task. When disputing parties can find an area of agreement or a subject where the disagreement is not as severely polarized, they are much better able to move toward resolution.

Picard (1998) offers that "Reframing is a rewording technique which puts issues in terms that both parties understand, and which leads them in the direction of a win-win solution. It is used to:

- Emphasize a positive goal
- Emphasize common ground
- Identify underlying needs
- Eliminate accusations or blaming
- Expand to the fuller meaning of a message
- Shift positional statements to issue or interest statements" (p. 71)

3. **No Favoritism:**

   A mediator needs to avoid being perceived as favoring one disputant or position over the other. One way a mediator can avoid accusations of favoritism is to ensure that their physical position—whether sitting or standing—is equidistant from each disputant, and that they maintain equal eye contact with both parties.

Mediators should also choose their words carefully when responding to compliments from disputants during the mediation. While some disputants may be sincere, others may be attempting to manipulate the situation. To maintain neutrality, mediators should refrain from gestures such as nodding in agreement or using phrases like "I see" or "I see your point." These subtle cues may lead one disputant to believe that the mediator is taking sides.

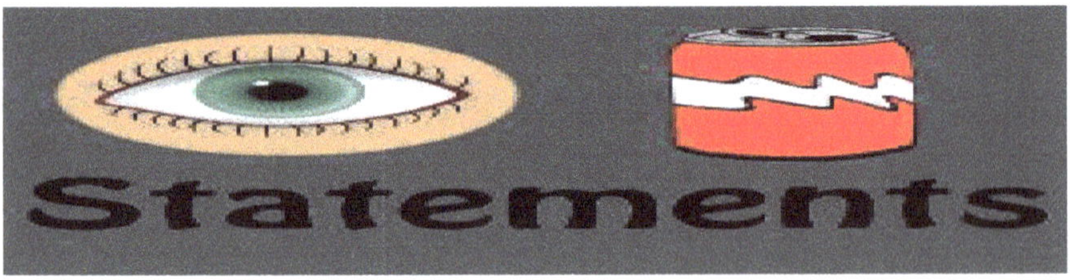

4. **"I" Statements:**

   Since beginning a sentence with "you" can sometimes have an accusatory tone, try to use "I" rather than "you" when addressing some disputants. However, simply placing an "I" at the beginning of a sentence is not necessarily sufficient. If the I-statement focuses on the other person's faults, it may be no different from a you-statement.

Essentially, I-statements should express what the mediator needs to happen. For example: "I need your cooperation."

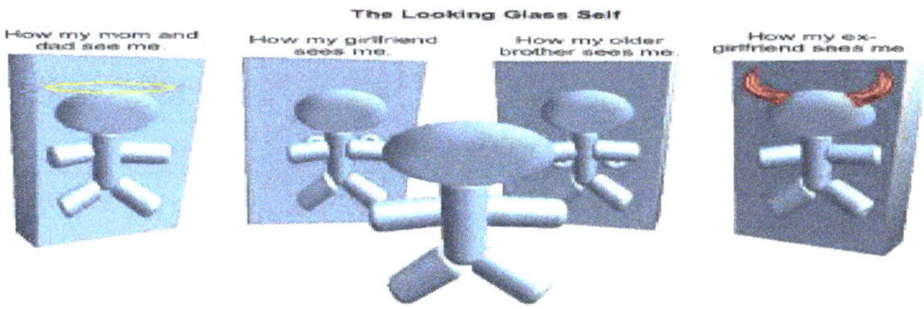

5. **Symbolic Interactionism:**

   Be aware of the symbols your body language communicates. Your stance or facial expressions may unintentionally escalate a dispute. Likewise, try to observe and interpret the body language of the disputants. This can help you gather valuable information about the nature and dynamics of the dispute.

Nonverbal Messages:

Nonverbal communication occurs through three primary channels of expression:

1. **Proxemics** – Spatial relationships and their influence on communication. Examples include office design, the type and style of furniture, seating arrangements, and the physical distance separating all parties.
2. **Kinesics** – Body language; all forms of physical movement.
3. **Paralinguistics** – The vocal components of a message other than the actual words, including pace, pitch, tone, and volume (Kovach, 2004, p. 55).

The mediator must be attentive to both parts of a message: the content (the substantive portion) and the affective component (the emotional or feeling part) (Kovach, 2004).

Caveat:

The mediator should acknowledge the individual's feelings but must be careful not to focus too heavily on the emotional aspect of the message. Mediation is not a therapy session (Kovach, 2004). The mediator's primary role is to keep the process goal-oriented and avoid attempting to fix problems or provide counseling. Doing so could cause the mediator to slip into a sympathetic rather than empathetic role, making them part of the problem rather than a neutral facilitator helping to resolve the dispute.

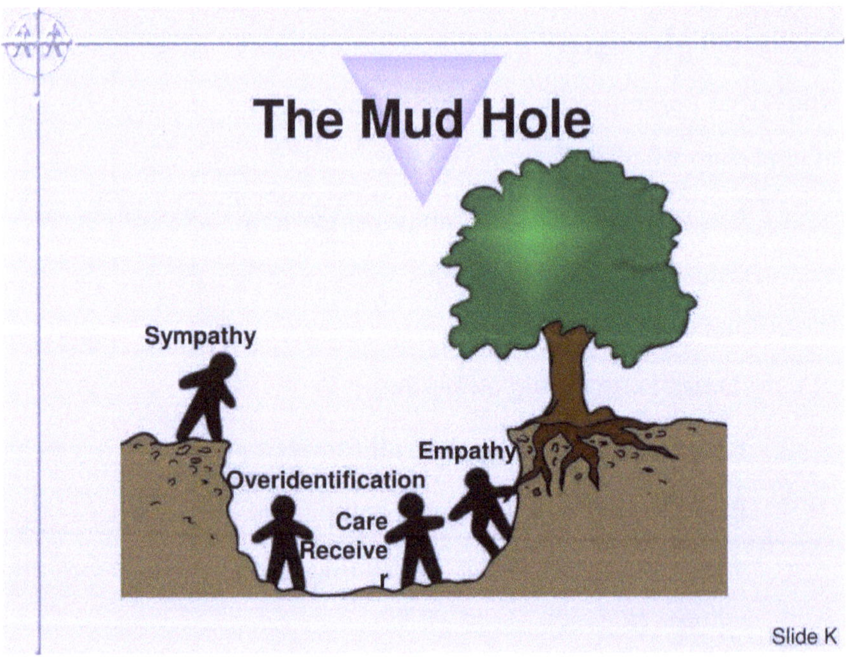

Eliminate Stereotypes

6. Eliminate Stereotypes

One of the most controversial issues in society is the stereotyping of people, industries, countries, professions, and vocations. These topics often lead to misinterpretations, phobias, polarization, and a lack of understanding. This subjectivity fosters fear, mistrust, and a loss of respect, which results in the spread of false narratives and perspectives.

- **People:** This includes a wide range of personal, genetic, and medical attributes such as gender, sexual orientation, race, ethnicity, and infirmities that might cause fear, discomfort, or a lack of acceptance by those who are adverse to these topics.
- **Industries:** Many industries have been scrutinized for the solicitation of products and their overall purpose and effectiveness, which has led to questioning the validity of both the product and the industry.

- **Countries:** Every country has a culture that may differ in social values, such as faiths, beliefs, customs, traditions, intellectual grounding, and laws. Therefore, it is important for a mediator to be aware of cultural differences and avoid stereotyping them. This awareness helps the mediator understand each party's perspective and reasoning, which is essential to keeping the mediation process goal-oriented.
- **Professions:** Every profession includes individuals who fail to uphold the oaths or mission statements that obligate them to act responsibly and be accountable to those they serve and by whom they are employed. When some fail to do so, the image of the entire profession may be tarnished, inviting criticism and stereotyping.
- **Vocations:** Although professions and vocations often overlap, it is necessary to distinguish the two. Vocations are chosen by individuals who feel called to serve others. They do not pursue the work for monetary gain, but out of a sense of duty. Still, as with professions, some individuals serving in vocations have discredited themselves and their field, leading to public distrust and stereotyping of others who remain faithful to their calling.

Stereotyping is a harmful and degrading assumption rooted in misinformation often propagated through social, political, and media platforms. Mediators must be consciously aware of these tendencies and resist surrendering to them psychologically. Avoid making assumptions or using stereotypes when assessing parties in a dispute. Be proactive in dispelling them.

Randolph (2016) notes, "Our perceptions and assumptions are inevitably influenced by our prejudices and biases. These biases will in turn have been created because of our own past experiences or adopted from what we have heard or seen in others. They may result from social, economic, or ethnic identification, because we tend to categorize ourselves into groups. In so doing we immediately differentiate ourselves from other groups, and this can result in polarization and the 'Us and Them' experience" (p. 107). Gender-based tendencies, such as the expression of emotion, can influence how the mediation process is conducted. Gender may also impact how parties negotiate.

Culture:

Culture requires more in-depth examination, as it can be a root cause of conflict. Kovach (2004) explains, "The importance of a mediator's knowledge of culture and its impact on the parties and their representatives is twofold" (p. 72).

One: Conflict might arise from a party's misunderstanding or misinterpretation of events or issues they have witnessed or been involved in. A party may not fully understand what they are witnessing, causing concern, alarm, fear, or anger due to misinterpretation. Conversely, the party alleged to have caused the concern may not understand the reason for the reaction. Mediators must be aware of cultural characteristics that may contribute to communication challenges between the parties or with the mediator.

Two: Mediators must possess strong awareness of cultural diversity to facilitate communication and understanding that keeps the mediation process goal-oriented. Mediators should remain neutral and respect cultural differences, using peacebuilding methods that are appropriate to the nature of the dispute. Hass et al. (2017) remind us, "We are all different in some way, and our ideas and opinions will often disagree" (p. 398).

Kovach (2004) emphasizes the significance of cultural norms in determining the resolution of a dispute. Variations in cultural values may influence the type of resolution that will be acceptable. For instance, in some cultures, an apology or a handshake may suffice. Native Americans may acknowledge their role in a conflict as part of the resolution process. Ultimately, the parties involved decide what type of resolution is appropriate, and the mediator's cultural competence is vital in ensuring the process remains effective and goal-oriented.

7. Introspecting (Flip Siding – Self-Reflection)

Sometimes mediators need to step into another person's shoes—not to agree with them, but to better understand what they are experiencing. Through self-reflection, a mediator may ask, *What would I do or think if I were experiencing what this party is going through?* This process ties into symbolic interactionism. The ability to interpret symbolic messages enables us to take on the role of others.

This role-taking involves imagining ourselves in the other person's position, then evaluating how that person might be thinking and feeling and anticipating what actions they might take. Such reflection can provide valuable insight for the mediator during the brainstorming phase of mediation.

It is important to distinguish between sympathy, empathy, and understanding:

- **Sympathy** is feeling sorry for someone.
- **Empathy** allows us to communicate our comprehension of a person's feelings.
- **Understanding** is knowing the difference between sympathy and empathy.

8. Transforming Disputes

Transforming a raw dispute into a manageable form without causing total chaos is a vital role of the mediator. By reshaping the dispute into something manageable, the mediator helps prevent shouting and assists the parties in framing the issues and putting the conflict into perspective.

Remember that when some people are involved in an interpersonal dispute, they may scream, curse, and behave dramatically. They might begin arguing with each other as soon as they walk into the mediation room. In such situations, the mediator must take control. However, it is important not to take it personally—very rarely is their aggression or anger directed at the mediator.

If the mediator is intervening in a dispute already in progress (an informal mediation), it may be helpful to allow the parties a moment to vent. In most cases, they will calm down afterward.

Chapter 5

Mediation Values

Professional Mediator Qualities

The mediator needs to create a positive environment that encourages trust and respect. Kovach (2004) suggests that mediators need to set up guidelines that will help achieve a positive environment. I use humanistic values that include kindness, care, and empathy. Here are some guidelines I suggest for how the mediator can create a positive environment:

- Convey sincere acknowledgment of feelings
- Arrange for a secure setting
- Allow parties to vent (within clear limits)
- Cease hostile venting
- Speak softly and calmly
- Furnish facial tissue
- When appropriate, employ a light touch on the arm

• Elicit and explore personal viewpoints and perspectives on feelings to empower the parties to proceed past the emotions

• Avoid becoming emotionally involved

• Continue to be objective and neutral

Human Behavior, Motivation, and Persuasion – The Mediator's Role

Human behavior is predicated on needs. Everyone has them; however, their inspiration for achieving those needs varies by individual motives or interests. Therefore, it is important that the mediator utilize their skills to discern these needs or interests.

When parties are first introduced to the mediation process, they are often filled with anger and hostility toward each other. It is therefore incumbent upon the mediator to uncover the underlying issues that cause such anger and hostility in order to mitigate their intensity. A mediator's focus is to identify the underlying needs in order to keep the process goal-oriented toward reconciliation. However, this is not always an easy task, especially when emotions escalate.

The mediator must remain mentally alert to their own preconceived opinions and embrace an open-minded perspective—a neutral position. A mediator is a third-party neutral, which is a core value of the profession. The mediator's role is guided by the following precepts:

• Expect diversity to ensure a respectful process

- Be a good listener
- Distinguish underlying interests
- Do not prejudge the outcome of the mediation
- Empower the disputants—it is their conflict to resolve, not the mediator's

Mediation Skills

A successful mediator needs to possess several skills, including but not limited to:

- Empathy
- Creativity
- Critical thinking
- Coaxing and organizational skills
- Messaging
- Methodical thinking
- Self-restraint
- Ability to control the process
- Substantial knowledge

Mediation is an interdisciplinary field. Mediators come from all walks of life. Each mediator is an individual with a unique variety of life experiences and personality that must be used in conjunction with the mediation process (Kovach, 2004, p. 51).

The Role of a Mediator

The mediator's role is that of a facilitator, but how one facilitates differs. Some of the roles include:

- Traffic cop: directing the communication
- Conductor
- Supervisor
- Parent
- Teacher
- Clarifier
- Advocate
- Catalyst: moving the parties in the direction of resolution
- Orchestrator
- Dealmaker
- Translator

There is considerable concern about the degree of influence the mediator should have on the outcome of the case and, to some degree, the process itself. Thus, the mediator needs to continually practice awareness of maintaining neutrality while remaining in control of the process. The parties are responsible for the content; the mediator is responsible for the process (Kovach, 2004, p. 45).

The Role of Trust

The development, repair, and maintenance of trust among all mediation participants are critical aspects of the process. At the essence of trust is the impact it has on relationships. Trust, or its absence, is a key element.

It is essential that the mediator establish trust with the parties in order for them to feel comfortable sharing information, especially private or personal matters. The parties must also trust the strategies the mediator employs.

Trust has two distinct forms:

One: Calculus-Based Trust – A decision to trust—or not—is made based on fear of violating trust as well as the perceived value or reward of maintaining it. This is an ongoing and calculated assessment.

Two: Identification-Based Trust – This is based on individuals identifying with one another and is more relational in nature, especially within personal relationships.

A lack of trust can impede any progress in mediation. Mediators must address trust issues on two levels:

One: Many parties come to mediation with a relationship in which trust has been damaged or does not exist. In order to reach mutual agreement, they must regain some level of confidence in the other party. The mediator should identify what kind of trust previously existed and help to repair it if possible.

Two: When parties did not have a prior relationship and trust never existed, the mediator may want to focus on the potential for establishing trust. Doing so can increase both the likelihood of reaching an agreement and subsequent compliance with it.

Trust is closely related to confidentiality in mediation. Establishing trust between participants and the mediator is central to the process. Only when trust is present will people disclose important information and personal needs.

Parties may be hesitant to engage in settlement negotiations if they fear something they say could be used against them in a future trial. With confidentiality assured, parties and attorneys are more willing to discuss all matters openly and propose settlements. Offers to compromise disputed claims, as well as settlement agreements, have traditionally been inadmissible in court to prove liability. This exclusion is supported by two reasons: lack of relevance and the policy favoring settlements (Kovach, 2004, pp. 173–175).

Ethical Considerations

Mediator Ethics

There is a built-in inconsistency in the development of standards for mediators. A basic premise of mediation is its flexibility. That flexibility is one of mediation's key benefits. There are no definitive standards of mediator competency, nor would traditional testing for mediators be advisable (Kovach, 2004, p. 396).

Current Codes

Currently, there are likely over a hundred separate codes of mediator ethics, many of which include standards of conduct. A mediator's duties may vary depending on the type of case, the mediator's background, the agency in which the case is mediated, or the place of referral, such as a court (Kovach, 2004, p. 399).

Areas for Ethical Consideration

The main topics of mediator ethics include:

1. Conflicts of interest
2. Neutrality
3. Role of the mediator
4. Party self-determination
5. Quality of process
6. Qualifications
7. Providing professional advice
8. Confidentiality
9. Advertising and fees
10. Duties in the profession

(Kovach, 2004, p. 402)

Chapter 6

the Mediation Process Outline

Mediation Steps

Step 1: Opening Statement

Step 2: Tell Issues / Uninterrupted Time

Each side conveys their version of the events.

Step 3: Mediator Clarifies

The mediator reiterates and articulates key points conveyed by each side and asks probing questions.

Step 4: Brainstorming / Generating Possible Resolutions (Cross Talk)

Step 5: Agreement

Seating

Seating is an important aspect of the mediation process. Prior to the parties entering the venue where the mediation will take place, the furniture where they and the mediator(s) will be sitting needs to be arranged.

The major concern regarding seating is that the venue provides an atmosphere of equality, safety, and professionalism. Therefore, there should be a table large enough to facilitate seating for the parties to comfortably sit across from cach other, with the mediator(s) positioned between them at the head or end of the table.

In a co-mediation process, the mediators may sit together or at opposite ends of the table.

It is important to note a few significant visual considerations. First, the setting and appearance of the chairs used by the mediator and the parties should be of the same material and design. Second, inform the parties prior to seating so they may choose where they would like to sit. This may serve as the mediator's first opportunity to empower the parties. Third, the mediator should position their chair in a location that allows easy access to the exit. This is for safety reasons.

Chapter 7

Step One

Opening Statements

Explanation of:

- Mediation
- BATNA (Best Alternative to a Negotiated Agreement)
- Agreement Authority
- Note Taking
- Confidentiality
- Identifying Ground Rules (tailor the ground rules for your audience)
- Caucus

Explanation of Mediation

The mediator's introductory remarks can establish the tone and tenor of the entire mediation session. The introduction is the primary vehicle through which the mediator begins to build trust with the participants. The mediator can set the stage for the session by exhibiting an enthusiastic, positive, and encouraging attitude.

Following are some specific items that should be included:

Purpose

The purpose of the mediator's introduction is to inform the participants about what is going to happen. The mediator can use this introductory time to provide the parties an opportunity to relax and feel more at ease with the surroundings, the mediator, and the process. This is also the time during which the mediator can set the tone and let the participants know that they are in control of the mediation process.

Opening Remarks

It is time to hear from the participants. The focus will be on the nature of the dispute; however, the dispute may not be what the mediator assumes it is. The mediator must be careful not to bring into the session any presumptions about the case based on information previously received. The mediator should stress this to the parties as a way of encouraging each person to listen to the others.

The discussions are not limited to the nature of the case but are open to all areas of controversy between the parties. These areas may include the primary and underlying causes of the conflict, as well as tangential issues and interests.

Importance of Opening Remarks

The mediation is often the first opportunity that the disputing parties have to express what the problem is, as they see it. No one should interrupt the speaker during the time reserved for opening remarks. During the opening remarks, the mediator may take notes while listening to what is said. The mediator should look for areas of agreement among the parties, as well as note matters of perceived disagreement. Emphasize perceptions.

Parties

The mediation is often perceived as the individual's day in court, and it should be treated as such. Ventilation—the expression of anger, frustration, and other emotions—is a part of the mediation process and should be encouraged, within limits. The mediator should be careful not to allow venting to become a direct attack on the other side. If the venting becomes destructive, the mediator can caucus.

Mediators need to remember that this may be the first time a participant is involved in a mediation process. Thus, the mediator needs to teach the participant about proper procedures (Kovach, 2004, pp. 158–160).

Attorneys

Ordinarily, when an attorney attends a mediation, there is a lawsuit pending. It is important that the mediator determine the status or stage of the lawsuit in advance. Lawyers should be careful not to use the opening statement at mediation as they would an opening or closing argument at trial. Instead, they should use the time to set forth the specifics of the case.

The mediator should refrain from requesting specific offers from the lawyers. Specifying goals too early in the process often results in inflexibility. Lawyers should not further aggravate the conflict. General statements about goals and outcomes of the session can be encouraged by the mediator (Kovach, 2004, p. 165).

Use of Documents, Witnesses, and Experts

In complex cases, a party and their representative may use documents, witnesses, and experts to clarify certain points. These are adjustments to the process and should be kept to a minimum. Mediation is not a fact-finding or adjudicative process. Each party in the case should be given an opportunity to complete their initial remarks. Additional information from outsiders should be avoided at the initial stage (Kovach, 2004, p. 167).

A Reiteration of the Importance of the Mediation Process

A neutral third party (mediator):

- Assists disputants in resolving a conflict or dispute
- Does not impose a decision

- Listens to the disputants
- Helps identify issues
- Keeps the mediation goal-directed for disputants to create their own resolution

A third party assists disputants in resolving matters of disagreement between themselves. The mediator is an active and assertive facilitator but does not impose a decision. The mediator assists the disputants in fashioning their own agreement.

The mediator's role is to set the stage for mediation, listen to the disputants, help them frame the issues, and keep the mediation goal-directed so the parties can create their own resolution.

The mediation process is a win-win process. Win-win applies because each disputant agrees to the resolution and was an integral player in fashioning it. Parties to a dispute collectively work out a compromise.

Specifically:

- Disputants fashion their own agreement
- Mediator does not impose a decision
- This is not a court
- The mediator is not a judge

BATNA – Best Alternative to a Negotiated Agreement

Times when BATNA becomes an issue:

1. In talking with disputants in pre-mediation meetings, a BATNA analysis is helpful in determining if mediation is the best alternative
2. Attempting to show a party why it is to their advantage to participate in mediation
3. For a variety of reasons (e.g., at an impasse), while the mediation is underway, the mediator may want to remind the parties of what may happen if the mediation is not successful

BATNA is the key focus and driving force behind a successful negotiator. Disputants should not accept a resolution worse than their BATNA.

Agreement Authority

How binding is the agreement? The agreement is the same as a contract wherein all contractual laws are invoked. It is a binding legal contract, provided the parties are at least 18 years old.

Where Can a Disputant Get Enforcement if the Agreement is Breached?

Instructions for Breached Agreements:

In the event that an agreement is breached—that is, if the other person does not follow through with the agreement—a disputant is encouraged to contact the Mediation Center. If the Center cannot assist, it is suggested that the disputant contact the State's Attorney's Office or the Civil Court.

Telephone at least one of the mediators who handled the case:

Name: _______________

Telephone: _______________

Name: _______________

Telephone: _______________

If you are unsuccessful in contacting a mediator, then call the Center's main number.

Note Taking

Note-taking and organization during mediation varies from individual to individual. In complex cases, it is very important that notes be taken. However, note-taking must not become a distraction.

The most important element of nonverbal communication is eye contact. The mediator may find it difficult to maintain eye contact with the speaker while taking copious notes. Therefore, use short phrases and abbreviations.

Mediators should be aware that individuals react differently to note-taking.

A mediator will find that as they progress in the process, experimentation with different methods will assist in finding the right balance.

Special care should be taken in noting the specific proposals and counterproposals made by the parties during the mediation (Kovach, 2004, pp. 61–62).

You need to write less than you think for the sake of your clients or employees:

- There's something about the mediator sitting with a notepad and pen that conveys "interview," "interrogation," or "record for your HR file."
- Mediation is one of the few places in people's lives where they have a chance to be truly listened to. Giving someone your undivided attention is a rare gift.

And you need to write less than you think for the sake of your own effectiveness as a mediator or coach.

When you're taking notes, you're multitasking. You are trying to do at least two things at once: write and listen. But when you're trying to do two things at once, your brain is switching between each task—back and forth, back and forth. One task gets attention while the other does not, and then the roles reverse as your attention switches again. Psychologists have a term, "switch costs," which refers to the cost of attention loss and the demands on willpower.

The bottom line? When you're writing, you're not fully listening. And that means you're missing things.

Sometimes what you're missing is a gem you should not have missed. That's a high price to pay for a crutch-habit.

Notes Destroyed

Confidentiality is critical to the success of the mediation process so that all persons attending can trust that they can have a full and frank discussion with the mediator about the issues. The mediator will present a Confidentiality Agreement to be signed by all persons attending the mediation.

The mediator will not report what happens in the privacy of a mediation session to anyone not in attendance, and nothing that is said in the session can be used later in arbitration or a court proceeding. All notes taken by the mediator will be destroyed after the mediation. Persons in attendance are free to retain their own notes. The only information that is not confidential is whether an agreement was reached, and if so, the terms of that agreement.

Confidentiality

Rule 408 – Compromise and Offers to Compromise

(a) Prohibited Uses. Evidence of the following is not admissible—on behalf of any party—either to prove or disprove the validity or amount of a disputed claim or to impeach by a prior inconsistent statement or a contradiction:

(1) furnishing, promising, or offering—or accepting, promising to accept, or offering to accept—a valuable consideration in compromising or attempting to compromise the claim; and

(2) conduct or a statement made during compromise negotiations about the claim—except when offered in a criminal

case and when the negotiations relate to a claim by a public office in the exercise of its regulatory, investigative, or enforcement authority.

(b) Exceptions. The court may admit this evidence for another purpose, such as proving a witness's bias or prejudice, negating a contention of undue delay, or proving an effort to obstruct a criminal investigation or prosecution (Kovach, 2004, p. 269).

In today's mediation climate, not all things are confidential. A mediator may have a duty to disclose certain matters discussed in mediation.

Confidentiality Agreements

Another means to secure confidentiality in mediation is through a confidentiality agreement. In non-litigation matters, it is likely that courts would enforce a confidentiality agreement unless other laws mandating disclosure take precedence.

Even in instances where enforcement by a court is questionable, there may be benefit in executing a nondisclosure agreement. The written agreement may serve as a deterrent. Individuals may maintain confidentiality because they have agreed to, not because they are legally bound to (Kovach, 2004, pp. 272–273).

Note-taking is a confidential process. The mediator and disputants may take notes, but the notes are destroyed at the end of the mediation. If notes are kept, then only the mediator may retain them, and only for the purpose of becoming part of a confidential record. This record (notes) is not admissible in a court of law.

Example of a Confidentiality Agreement

This process is confidential. Anything said in the process is not to be repeated outside the process. Exceptions:

1. General characteristics of the case
2. Whether an agreement was reached or not
3. The contents of the agreement

Confidentiality extends to any conversations that the mediator may have with anyone other than their colleagues from the XYZ Mediation Center. The mediator will not discuss particulars (anything said in the mediation that is not in the agreement) with the State's Attorney or their representatives, or members of the judiciary. Moreover, the mediator should not be called to testify in a court of law about what they heard during the mediation process.

Name printed ____________________

Signature ____________________

Disputants must honor the confidentiality agreement at a minimum by agreeing not to repeat what is discussed in the mediation outside of the mediation, except to those who have a legal right to know (e.g., respective lawyers).

Identifying Ground Rules (Tailor the Ground Rules for Your Audience)

The best way to figure out what the ground rules are is to ask: When you are having a disagreement with someone, how do you expect that other person to behave toward you?

1. ______________________________
2. ______________________________
3. ______________________________
4. ______________________________
5. ______________________________
6. ______________________________
7. ______________________________

Please, whatever you do, do not forget to tailor the ground rules for your audience.

Examples only:

- No interruptions – one person speaks at a time
- No profanity
- No threats or intimidation
- No shouting
- No physical contact

The Caucus

The caucus describes that portion of the mediation session where the mediator meets privately with each party or combination of parties.

Benefits of Caucus

- Parties can be more candid
- Gather information
- Explore alternatives
- Allow a party to vent in private
- Can prevent one party from manipulating another
- Mediators can be more direct and prevent "losing face"
- Parties may be more willing to share sensitive information
- Mediator can educate participants
- Provides parties some "down time" to relax
- Mediator can address inappropriate behavior
- Mediators can do more "reality testing"

Caution and Concerns

- Use of caucus in community settings or when the disputing parties have an ongoing relationship
- Perception of alliance or bias
- Amount of time spent during a caucus
- Risk of mediator being manipulated

• Mediator could hear something they prefer not to know (Kovach, 2004, p. 239)

• A party (disputant) may call for a caucus

• A mediator may call for a caucus

• If a mediator calls for a caucus, they must caucus with both parties. This will be done with each disputant separately.

Mediation Referral

• Individual outreach

• Court

• Prosecutor

• Police

General Appropriateness

The specific factors that indicate a case or matter is appropriate for mediation are numerous. An illustrative listing includes the following:

• There is an ongoing relationship that the parties wish to maintain

• The parties hope to establish an ongoing relationship through the mediation

• The parties prefer to avoid a legal precedent

• There is a need for assurance of confidentiality about the nature of the dispute, the agreement, or both

• There exists a need for assistance in communication and information exchange

• The parties demonstrate an inability to identify common interests

• The parties and/or their advocates need assistance with the negotiation process

• There is a need for creativity in resolution

• The parties express a desire for self-determination

• One or both parties (or their counsel) have made an unrealistic assessment of the case• Despite differences, a mutual superordinate goal of attaining a mutually satisfactory resolution exists (Kovach, 2004, pp. 75–76)

The Referral Process

Non-Legalized Matters

These are disputes or conflicts that have not accessed the legal system.

• Voluntary

• Contractual

(Kovach, 2004, pp. 79–81)

Chapter 8

Step Two

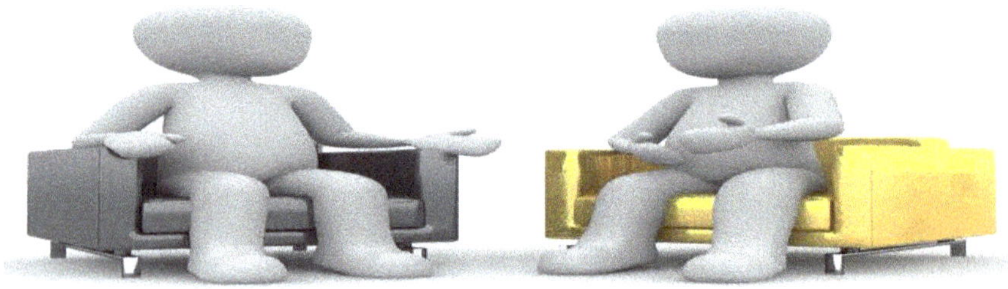

Tell Issues / Uninterrupted Time

• Systematic

• Rebuttals

• The TPI (mediator) should not function as an interviewer or fact finder

• The parties and/or their representatives are invited to make an uninterrupted presentation of their views of the dispute

• No interruptions

• Parties fully explain to the mediator and to each other, in their own words, how they view the dispute

• The mediator will engage the parties in an information-gathering process to provide a clear and complete picture of what the dispute is about

• The mediator should begin by asking open-ended questions

• The parties may need to express their feelings. Venting affords individuals an opportunity to release frustration, anger, and other emotions. If such emotions are not expressed, the dispute often cannot be resolved

Systematic

The mediator needs to ensure equality, free from bias and power imbalance between the disputants. There must be no favoritism on the part of the mediator. To help facilitate this, the mediator needs to determine a method for selecting who speaks first. Examples could include, but are not limited to, having disputants select a number that the mediator writes on a piece of paper. The disputant who guesses the number or comes closest to it speaks first. A coin toss may also be used.

When a mediator determines that a caucus is needed, the mediator will caucus individually with both disputants—first with one disputant, and upon completion, with the other.

Remember, the mediator is responsible for guiding the mediation and ensuring that each disputant is allowed an equal opportunity to tell their version of the conflict. The mediator will gently remind the disputants of any ground rule violations and will moderate a sustainable flow of the mediation process.

Neutrality

Neutrality is a central concept of mediation. The mediator is referred to as the third-party neutral. The mediator is expected to remain neutral throughout the mediation process—before, during, and after the session. Impartiality is key to the mediator's role.

Rebuttals

The mediator will ensure that each disputant has an opportunity to rebut, debunk, or debate issues that arise during the mediation process. The mediator will remind the disputants that they will be afforded equal opportunities to do so.

The TPI (Mediator) Should Not Function as an Interviewer or Fact Finder

Communication through Questioning

A caveat to questioning during a private session or caucus is confidentiality. Questions assist the parties in gaining clarification. Effective questioning is an important skill that has a significant impact on the mediation process (Kovach, 2004, p. 58).

The parties and/or their representatives are invited to make an uninterrupted presentation of their views of the dispute.

Setting the Agenda

The use of an agenda for further discussion can bring additional structure to the mediation process. Setting the agenda can be a strategic move for the mediator. Conflicts can be defined in ways that either magnify or minimize the dispute. The mediator should approach agenda-setting and the discussion of issues in a way that helps to minimize the dispute. If the mediator initiates discussion in a certain manner and finds it ineffective, it is appropriate to stop, rethink, reassess, and take a different approach.

There are several approaches to agenda-setting:

• Ad hoc – the mediator proposes examination of an issue as it is discussed

• Simple agenda – one main issue is taken for discussion

• Alternating choices by the parties – gives parties more control of the process

• Principled – the mediator, with the assistance of the parties, establishes general principles that form the framework for settlement

• Less difficult first – the mediator identifies those issues where the probability of agreement is high

• Most difficult first – closely related to the following approach of order of importance, particularly where there is agreement on the most important itcm

• Order of importance – the parties, with the mediator's assistance, choose the most important item for each of them

• Building-block or contingent agenda – the mediator identifies issues that must be addressed first, as they provide the groundwork or foundation for later decisions

• Tradeoff or packaging – parties unwilling to move on a single issue may use combinations of issues. Offers are made in return for concessions. The mediator orchestrates this exchange. Issues may be traded one for another in such a way that mutual bargaining results

The mediator will engage the parties in an information-gathering process to provide a clear and complete picture of what the dispute is about.

Follow-Up Information Gathering

Rarely in mediation sessions do the parties provide enough information during opening remarks to fully identify the issues and move directly into option generation. Information gathering is a significant stage of mediation and should not be overlooked or rushed.

Effective Questioning by the Mediator

The mediator should continue to gather more information from the participants. There are several reasons for this:

• Clarify and understand

• Focus on the main areas of contention

• Focus on areas of mutual or shared interest

• Obtain a more expansive view of the dispute

• Use open-ended questions to search for mutual agreement among the participants

• Use broad, open questions to elicit more detailed responses

• Distinguish between primary questions and probing questions—a primary question may be planned in advance and asks for an overview of the situation, while probing questions seek greater detail based on prior responses

(Kovach, 2004, p. 168)

The mediator should begin by asking open-ended questions.

An open-ended question is a form of qualitative inquiry. These questions are asked to establish a platform for better understanding. They allow the audience to express what is on their mind.

An open-ended question has no set limits as to duration, direction, amount, number, or content; it is broad, unlimited, or unrestricted. Such a question is designed to facilitate discussion or encourage a full, meaningful answer using the subject's own knowledge and feelings.

Examples of Mediation Questions

- What has this conflict done to your relationship?
- How has your desire to maintain family traditions affected your relationships with one another?

The Parties May Need to Express Their Feelings (Venting)

Allowing free expression of strong emotion provides individuals an opportunity to release frustration, anger, and other emotions. If such emotions are not expressed, the dispute often cannot be resolved.

Virtues of Venting

- In many (though not all) situations, it is better to discharge negative emotions than to keep them bottled up

• Venting helps restore emotional equilibrium

• When emotionally entangled, a person may struggle to think clearly about what actions remain available

• Ideally, individuals should be capable of moving beyond difficult emotions by reassessing the negative assumptions or judgments they have attached to others

• Directly confronting the source of frustration may carry serious risks, such as job loss or relationship breakdown

(Seltzer, 2014, p. 1)

Chapter 9

Step Three

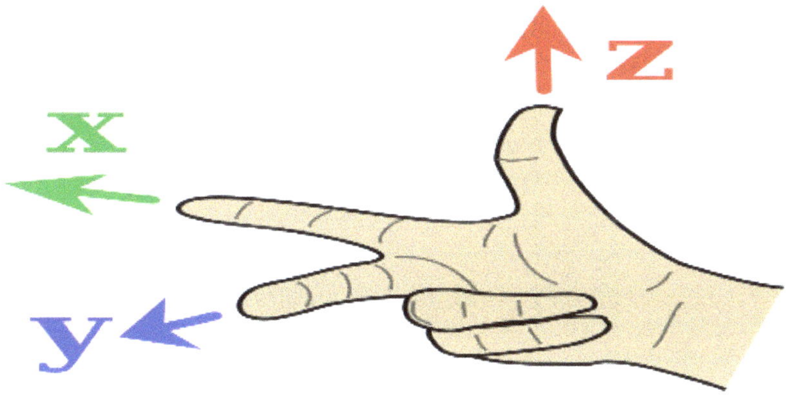

Mediator Clarifies

• The mediator clarifies, reiterates, and verbally articulates the issues in contention. This includes the mediator asking questions.

• Neutralizing

• Rephrasing

• Paraphrasing

• This may or may not involve identifying the underlying interests of the parties

• Once the mediator has identified the issues, they will move the parties toward generating ideas, options, or alternatives that might resolve the case

• It is during this time that the mediator may caucus

• It is advisable that some attempt at issue identification take place while the parties are together

The mediator clarifies, reiterates, and verbally articulates the issues in contention. This includes the mediator asking questions.

Neutralize:

Render (something) ineffective or harmless by applying an opposite force or effect.

Rephrase

To express an idea or question in an alternative way, especially with the purpose of changing the detail or perspective of the original idea or question.

Paraphrase

To express the meaning of the writer, speaker, or something written or spoken using different words, especially to achieve greater clarity.

Paraphrasing helps confirm whether the mediator accurately received the disputant's message. If the paraphrase is incorrect, the mediator will give the disputant an opportunity to correct the mediator.

Paraphrasing should take the form of questions that reveal the mediator's understanding while eliciting any necessary corrections from the disputant (Rosenberg, 2015).

The mediator will engage the parties in an information-gathering process to provide a clear and complete picture of what the dispute is about. Once the mediator is certain that enough information has been gathered, they should begin to identify the primary issues. During this phase, the mediator should also simultaneously attempt to identify the underlying interests of each party (Kovach, 2004, p. 179).

Issues

Issues are items that both sides are willing to openly discuss as the predominant points of contention, and about which the negotiation has been initiated. In most cases, each party also has certain underlying issues or interests. The mediator should initially focus on identifying and restating the primary, apparent issues.

At this stage of the process, and in the absence of overt hostility, the parties should remain together. When identifying the issues, there should be mutual agreement on what those issues are or, at a minimum, an acknowledged agreement to disagree. This may stimulate a need for a caucus (Kovach, 2004, p. 179).

- ❖ The purpose of Step Three is to ensure that the mediator and parties are clear about the matters in disagreement, as well as the positions and interests held by each disputant. Once the mediator has recited the issues to the satisfaction of all parties, the process moves to Step Four.

Chapter 10

Step Four

Brainstorming / Generating Possible Resolutions

• This is the give-and-take part of the mediation, where the mediator assists the parties in their bargaining by generating ideas.

• The mediator may engage in reality testing, which involves checking with each side the realistic possibility of achieving what they are hoping for. This will also help move them away from unrealistic positions.

Finding a Resolution

Once the mediator has identified the primary issues of the case, they restate them and obtain confirmation from the parties. Mediators begin to guide the parties toward identifying and generating a variety of options and alternatives that may lead to a final resolution. Mediators should keep in mind the parties' underlying interests. Rather than focusing on finding one specific answer or resolution, several alternative solutions should be considered. Mediators need to provide guidance and direction at this phase of the process.

An important benefit of mediation is that, through the process, participants can find and agree to alternative solutions. These solutions are generally more satisfactory to the disputants because they are crafted in a way that accomplishes at least some of the goals of both parties (Kovach, 2004, p. 236).

Overcoming Reluctance with Problem Solving

Most individuals do not consciously think of problem solving as a distinct, identifiable process. When they encounter a problem, a dispute, or an uncomfortable situation, their instinctive response is to try to find an answer. They often assume that there is a single solution to be found. This results in a narrow and restrictive focus.

Disputes exist because two or more people have different feelings, views, perspectives, and needs. When individuals look at the problem, each has their own idea for its solution. Collaboration in developing options does not come naturally to most people, particularly those involved in conflict.

The mediator's goal is to move the disputing parties away from searching for a single correct answer and to broaden their perspectives by reframing the disputed issues in broad terms.

An impediment to problem solving is the reluctance of the parties to share responsibility for a dispute and its resolution. The mediator must help the parties recognize that mediation is a collaborative problem-solving process.

In some cases, it is important that a wrong be acknowledged before a party can move forward. Mediators work with the parties to determine whether an apology can be part of the resolution. Attributing blame or responsibility for a past event is far less important than finding a solution that will work for both sides (Kovach, 2004, p. 237).

The Importance of Several Options

There are a variety of alternatives that might be suitable. This is particularly true in situations where the parties have multiple interests to be met. Therefore, before rushing to finalize a solution, the parties should explore several alternatives. The mediator facilitates this process and emphasizes that the parties should understand that any alternative, in whole or in part, may provide a workable solution to the problem (Kovach, 2004, p. 243).

Use of Lateral Thinking

In problem solving, our thinking should be slowed down. Immediate, automatic responses do not often produce creative options and solutions.

Lateral thinking is defined as pattern switching within a patterning system. It can be described as an attitude, as well as a set of methods or skills. At the very least, mediators must possess this attitude. Lateral thinking involves a new way of looking at issues and can be practiced as a re-patterning of how the mind works. It includes processes such as insight, creativity, and humor.

Lateral thinking is used for the generation of new ideas or invention. It is related to creativity but is more deliberate. It allows for jumps in different directions, and nothing should be excluded from consideration. With lateral thinking, the result is unpredictable at the beginning of the process. Therefore, especially in cases where creative solutions are needed, it is important that the mediator encourage the parties to employ lateral thinking (Kovach, 2004, pp. 246–247).

Brainstorming

The mediator facilitates a brainstorming session. During this process, it is acceptable to suggest alternatives, which the suggesting party may later reject. If judgment is suspended, the mediator will be better able to assist the parties in maximizing the available options. The mediator must also be careful not to reveal their own feelings or judgments about any of the suggestions and should remain focused on facilitating the process.

Approaches:

• Ad hoc: The mediator asks a general question and allows the participants to make suggestions. The ideas, without comment or further exploration, are then recorded by the mediator.

• Round robin: Each person takes a turn suggesting ideas. The process proceeds from person to person and may continue for several rounds.

• Slip method: Each person writes several different suggestions on slips of paper. The mediator, who may or may not participate, then lists the ideas without revealing who made each suggestion. None of the participants know who suggested which option (Kovach, 2004, pp. 248–249).

• The mediator facilitates brainstorming among disputants to generate solutions.

• Each disputant has a turn to name all the possible resolutions to the dispute.

• Ideally, each disputant can name even those resolutions that may not be the most favorable to them.

• The mediator listens for points of agreement.

• The mediator encourages dialogue on issues and possible resolutions.

• Again, the mediator listens for points of agreement.

• The mediator holds caucuses if necessary.

• The mediator may want to suggest solutions.

• The mediator verifies, reiterates, and verbally articulates the resolution reached.

Chapter 11

Step Five

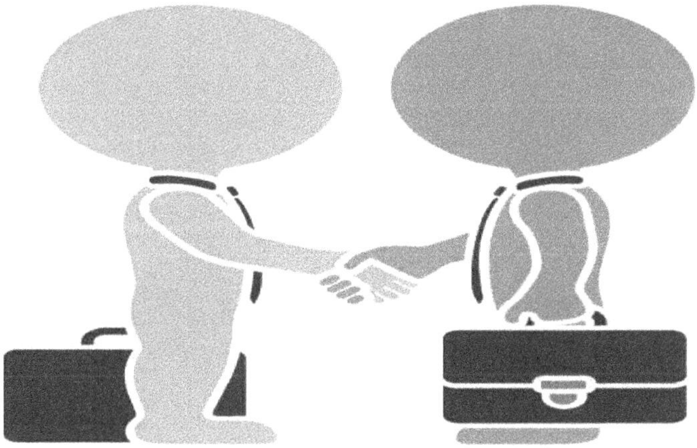

Agreement

• The mediator will restate the agreement.

• The mediator will draft either the complete agreement or a memorandum of settlement.

• If no agreement is reached, the mediator will restate where the parties stand.

The Mediated Agreement

A final agreement or resolution may not be reached in every mediation. Even in those cases that do not settle, the mediation can often be considered an achievement. Neither a mediation nor a mediator should be judged solely in terms of whether an agreement is reached. There are other factors to consider:

• The parties may discuss the case later and reach a final agreement

• There may be times when the parties end the session by agreeing to disagree

• Partial agreements are possible

• Agreements to reschedule the mediation

(Kovach, 2004, p. 339)

Finalizing the Mediated Agreement

It is the mediator's role and task to continue to guide the parties in concluding their agreement. The mediator should have notes identifying all the interests, issues, options, and agreements. It is important that they be an active participant in the formation of the agreement. The mediator should also ensure that all the items previously identified have either been addressed in the agreement or purposefully disregarded.

There are three important elements of a durable agreement:

• Procedural

• Psychological

• Substantive satisfaction

The mediator, when reaching the stage where the agreement becomes final, should determine from the parties, as much as possible, whether all three elements have been achieved, recognizing the overlap between them.

Procedural Satisfaction

Achieved by participation in the mediation. When each party has participated fully in the process or feels that they have been provided the opportunity to participate without pressure, they usually feel satisfied with the procedure.

Psychological Satisfaction

Will be present if the parties have not only had an opportunity to be heard but also to express their anger, frustration, disappointment, sadness, or other emotions.

Substantive Satisfaction

The mediator should take a directive role in determining the substance of the final agreement. Their role is not to dictate terms or specific content, but to ensure that all pertinent items are handled. It is impossible for a mediator to completely guarantee that all parties will be satisfied with the specific substance of an agreement. Nonetheless, if the mediator has identified the interests of each party and those interests are satisfied, the result will be an agreement with substantive satisfaction.

Where procedural, psychological, and substantive satisfaction are substantially achieved, it increases the likelihood that the parties will comply with the agreement (Kovach, 2004, pp. 340–341).

Contents of the Agreement

A mediation agreement does not have to be in writing, although when possible or feasible, it is best to memorialize an agreement in a written document.

Remember, an agreement is an official memorialization of what has been agreed to.

Benefits of written agreements include:

1. Less likelihood of disagreement as to what has been agreed to
2. In many cases, the agreement is a binding contract

Always write an agreement with as few legal terms as possible. Agreements should be reader-friendly to all people, not just those with legal expertise. When possible, use the words of the disputants. If the disputant states that they are sorry, you can write just that, or you could write the disputant's exact words (e.g., "I didn't mean what I did. I am really sorry.").

You must write an agreement in a way that the disputants can understand. The mediation agreement must explain one, some, or all of the following:

- **What**
- **When**
- **Where**
- **How**
- **Why**

What: What the agreement represents and what is going to happen or what is not going to happen.

When: When something (promised or agreed to) will happen. Make sure to specify dates if necessary.

Where: Where something will or will not happen.

How: How something will happen or how someone will do something.

Why: Why something will happen (e.g., to make a person whole again, as in rationale for restitution).

Remember that agreements are not confidential. Check with disputants as to what they do not want in an agreement after you have provided informed consent (that is, you have told them that agreements are not confidential).

Before writing the agreement formally, write a draft in the presence of the disputants if possible. Realize that as you move from Step 5 into Step 6, it is very likely that disputants will have second thoughts, remember things they had forgotten, or desire to clarify what they meant.

Go through the draft with the disputants to make sure that the agreement is exactly what they say they want. You must ensure that the agreement you write is an accurate reflection of what the disputants say is their resolution. If you do not, you have violated an ethical guideline in the practice of mediation.

Always have a dictionary with you so that you can refer to it when writing an agreement.

Before the disputants leave, once again explain to them how to address a breach of the agreement should one occur.

- The mediator specifies points of agreement as they understand them
- The mediator asks disputants to indicate if the agreement, as the mediator understands it, is accurate
- The agreement is memorialized in a written document. (If written, try to write the agreement in the disputants' own words.)
- The mediator explains that if there is a breach, the parties can go to court to have the agreement enforced, but the parties should consider returning to mediation

Partial Agreements

A mediator must keep in mind that, like all other stages of the process, the stage of finalizing the agreement must be flexible. This includes flexibility in the conclusion. In mediation, it is possible that instead of a complete settlement of the case, there will be one or more partial agreements.

Partial agreement is also possible in multi-party cases where there is complete agreement among some parties but not all of them.

The second type of partial agreement is a statement of a general intent to agree, or an agreement in principle, which leaves specific details to be worked out later.

The mediator should be able to recognize, identify, and clarify a partial agreement. The mediator will often outline it for the parties. In cases of partial agreements, the parties, after a period, may obtain additional information, see things differently, and wish to reschedule the mediation (Kovach, 2004, p. 346).

Form of the Agreement

The mediated agreement can take several forms. These range from the least formal, an oral agreement, to the most formal, a formalized legal document. The form of the agreement will often depend on the nature of the case and whether a lawsuit is pending.

Another informal type of agreement is an agreement in principle. The parties arrive at a general agreement, which includes further details that need to be worked out later.

If written, the agreement is usually in general outline form, in simple straightforward language, laying out what the parties have agreed to do (Kovach, 2004, p. 346).

Mediation as Facilitated Negotiation

A critical element of the mediator's role is to first diagnose, if possible, why the parties were unable to reach a resolution or settlement through direct negotiation.

Drafting Issues

The mediator plays a primary role in drafting the document, particularly in the physical production of the agreement (Kovach, 2004, p. 349).

Acknowledgments and Apologies

Apologies are usually offered when someone assumes some responsibility for their actions. An apology has been defined as a speech act given to someone. While originally an excuse or justification for one's actions, it has evolved to contain remorse and regret. Apologies may also be impacted by culture and experience and are at the basis of relationships.

MEDIATION AGREEMENT

PARTICIPANTS

Name (Printed)	Signature	Date
______________________	______________________	_________
______________________	______________________	_________

MEDIATOR

Mediator Name (Printed)	Signature	Date
______________________	______________________	_________

MEDIATION AGREEMENT

CO - MEDIATION

PARTICIPANTS

Name (Printed)	Signature	Date
____________________	____________________	__________
____________________	____________________	__________

ADDITIONAL SIGNATORIES (if applicable)

Name (Printed)	Signature	Date
____________________	____________________	__________
____________________	____________________	__________

MEDIATORS

Mediator Name (Printed)	Signature	Date
____________________	____________________	__________
____________________	____________________	__________

INSTRUCTIONS FOR BREACHED AGREEMENTS

If this agreement is breached, that is, if the other person does not follow through with the agreement, you are encouraged to contact the Mediation Center. If the Center cannot assist you, it is suggested that you contact the State's Attorney's Office or the civil court.

Telephone at least one of the mediators who handled your case:

Name: ______________________

Phone Number: ______________________

Name: ______________________

Phone Number: ______________________

If you are unsuccessful in contacting your mediator, then call the Center's main number:

XXX-XXX-XXXX

If you must leave a voice message, please make sure to specify that you are calling about a **BREACH**.

REFER – BACK FORM

The following case is not amenable to mediation or facilitation:

The parties were unable to come to an agreement:

Remarks if any:

____

____

____

____

Mediator: ____________________

Mediator: ____________________

Chapter 12

Psychological Aspects in Mediation

Counseling and Calming Skills

Many people in society seek punishment, revenge, retribution, and vendetta for perceived and real harms, whether physical or emotional. Thus, it is often difficult to persuade people to seek alternative measures to achieve justice and closure. To further exacerbate the issue, people who follow this paradigm of justice want to be vindicated, proven right, compensated, and to win their side of an argument or offense.

The mediator is often confronted by disputants who possess this psychological phenomenon, making it difficult to convince them that mediation is an appropriate mitigation process that allows both parties to win.

"In order to be of assistance to the parties, the mediator needs fully to understand the precise psychological influence that this strong desire to triumph has over the mediation process. To win, a party has four essential needs that must be satisfied:

- The need for vindication – to be proved right
- The need for revenge – for the other party to feel the same or similar pain
- The need for humiliation – for the other party to be shamed
- The need for compensation – to recover perceived losses"

(Randolph, 2016, p. 117)

This is when the mediator's skills, methods, and mental acumen are truly challenged. One could read research articles and books describing psychological behavior to gain knowledge and methods for addressing these complex issues. However, I challenge all mediators to internalize what I propose to be the underlying source that provides sustainable skills and methods for the mediation process and for working with those whose minds are focused on these issues: the heart.

From the Heart

Most mediations are the result of referrals. Thus, the mediator does not have prior knowledge of the disputants. Nonetheless, the mediator needs to possess some basic humanistic values—one of which, and the most important of all humanistic skills, is having heart. In fact, humanistic skills are predicated on the amount of heart a mediator possesses.

Throughout my professional and personal interactions with people, I have found that the most important need for engaging in mitigation methods is to put your heart into the situation. Without heart, a mediator will never hear the underlying issues—the voices expressing needs, pleading for someone to pay attention and listen. It is more than empathy, and certainly not sympathy, but a total immersion into the dispute process: paying attention, becoming an instrument in facilitating the mediation through total connectedness.

Having heart means that you, the mediator, are releasing the energy of your desire to fix things by allowing a preternatural experience. By putting your heart into the mediation process, the words and wisdom necessary to facilitate the mediation and enable a transformative outcome will begin to flow.

Chapter 13

Important Issues

Impasse

Impasse Defined:

- **Disputants are unable to reach an agreement.**
- **Mutually harmful.**
- **Provides opportunities for problem solving.**
- **Provides insight that leads to progress.**

Impasse, and the Ways Beyond

There are some methods that the mediator may employ when it appears the mediation is stuck. Most involve changing the dynamics of the process. Some of these strategies are to be used alone, others in combination. If one doesn't work, try another. Some sample tools to get past a roadblock include the following:

- Change the focus of the topic
- Start over
- Divide or break
- Take a break
- Be silent
- Discover or remind parties of their BATNA (Best Alternative to a Negotiated Agreement) or WATNA (Worst Alternative to a Negotiated Agreement)
- Use words of encouragement
- Call a caucus
- Come back together
- Bring snacks
- See if partial agreement can be reached
- Suggest the use, in whole or in part, of another ADR process
- Use humor
- Turn to outside experts
- Call it quits

(Kovach, 2004, pp. 241–242)

Other Stake Holders

Stakeholders: Other stakeholders could include family members, co-workers, friends, or any party outside the conflict who could ultimately or consequently be affected by the outcome of the mediation process.

Moot Issues: Having little or no practical relevance, typically because the subject is too uncertain to allow a decision.

Face Saving: The preserving of one's reputation, credibility, or dignity. This is an important issue regarding the mediator’s cultural awareness, as many cultures differ in the propriety of their personal social interactions.

Power Imbalances: Power imbalances exist when there are asymmetrical relations of power among or between disputants. A power imbalance exists when one disputant has more control or influence over another disputant’s behavior than vice versa.

Irrational Conceding: Irrational conceding takes place when a disputant becomes frustrated, overwrought, or feels overwhelmed with the mediation process and concedes to all the terms offered by the other disputant.

Informal Mediation: Informal mediation represents mediation conducted in a systematic and logical manner, but without strict adherence to the steps of the mediation process (although the goal is still an agreement fashioned by the disputants) (Cooper, 1999, p. 8).

Client Privilege: Interestingly, courts have held that communications between a client and attorney are protected by the mediation privilege, even where there is a later dispute between the client and the lawyer regarding the effectiveness of a settlement agreement.

Cassel v. Superior Court, 51 Cal. 4th 113, 118, 244 P.3d 1080, 1084 (2011), held that mediation protection applied to communication between non-adverse parties. In a different situation, the Supreme Court of Appeals of West Virginia found that a lower court did not err in allowing a mediator to testify where a party later claimed that the settlement reached at mediation did not include terms added by the opposing party after mediation.

Riner v. Newbraugh, 211 W. Va. 137, 144, 563 S.E.2d 802, 809 (2002), notcd, however, that the mediator did not disclose confidential communications; he only testified to the terms he believed were agreed upon as part of the settlement.

Given the inconsistency between jurisdictions, parties must enter into a mediation understanding that not all communications and documents will necessarily be protected, particularly in pre-suit mediations. It is important to know the jurisdiction's rules or statutes on the subject, including whether a privilege exists, who holds the privilege, and what is required to waive it.

In addition, a mediation party will need to determine what information it wants to share and whether additional precautions or agreements are necessary to protect the information. If possible, the parties should agree to the scope of confidentiality or other protections (for example, no waiver of attorney-client privilege or work product protection if shared with the mediator only), as well as who may waive the protection and when, if ever.

Mediators Testifying in Court: It is possible that a mediator will be compelled to testify in court.

In *In re Daley*, 29 S.W.3d 915, 918 (Tex. App.–Beaumont 2000, orig. proceeding), the court interpreted Sections 154.053 and 154.073 of the Texas Civil Practice and Remedies Code narrowly and allowed the mediator's testimony into evidence. Daley wanted to have the testimony of his actions during a mediation protected by Sections 154.053 and 154.073.

The Court of Appeals held that Section 154.053 restricts only the disclosure of matters that occur during the "settlement process," and testimony that Daley left the mediation without the mediator's permission was allowed, as it was unrelated to the settlement process.

The Court further held at page 918 that "Section 154.073 is not so broad as to bar all evidence regarding everything that occurs at mediation from being presented to the trial court. Rather than a blanket confidentiality rule for participants, the statute renders confidential 'a communication relating to the subject matter of the dispute of any… dispute' made by a participant in an ADR procedure."

The Court then found that testimony as to the actions of a participant during mediation that did not involve the subject matter of the dispute was admissible.

Pressures to Settle: Most cases settle sooner or later. Mediation frequently moves "later" to "sooner." In those cases in which the parties appear to be unable to reach a final settlement, there is disagreement about the role of the mediator.

Each mediator must use their best judgment when evaluating the degree of pressure to exert on the parties in advocating settlement. As a rule, where guidance is limited, the mediator must recall that their role is to assist the parties in arriving at their own settlement.

Problems in Generating Alternatives: The mediator's task is to create an environment where the parties are no longer reluctant to generate or identify a variety of options for settlement. The mediator will also encourage them to be willing to explore and consider those ideas suggested by the other parties at the mediation table.

Chapter 14

Preparation for the Mediator

Example of a Referral Form

Your dispute is being referred to the XYZ Mediation Center. The Mediation Center has trained mediators. Mediators are individuals who help people resolve interpersonal disputes like the one in which you may be involved. This is a free service for you.

A representative from the Mediation Center will receive part of the form. The representative will contact you (and the other person or people involved) within approximately 72 hours to arrange for your problem to go to mediation.

If questions arise before the notification, please contact the Mediation Center by email or phone.

The Referral Process

Non-Legalized Matters: Those disputes or conflicts which have not accessed the legal system are typically:

- Voluntary
- Contractual

(Kovach, 2004, pp. 79–81)

In a private mediation practice, the mediator often dictates the nature of the preparation. The mediator's preparation should begin by asking and answering two basic questions:

1. What do you, as the mediator, want the participants to know about the process and about you prior to sitting down at the mediation table?
2. What do you want to know about the case and the participants prior to beginning the mediation session?

Preparation is both mechanical and mental. Mechanical preparation involves logistics, housekeeping, and administrative details (Kovach, 2004, p. 143). Conduct the session in a neutral location.

§ 3182. Authority of Mediators; Exclusion of Counsel; Exclusion of Domestic Violence Support Person

(a) The mediator has authority to exclude counsel from participation in the mediation proceedings pursuant to this chapter if, in the mediator's discretion, exclusion of counsel is appropriate or necessary.

(b) The mediator has authority to exclude a domestic violence support person from a mediation proceeding as provided in Section 6303.

(Kovach, 2004, p. 149)

Chapter 15
Benefits of a TPI

1. Identifying Issues or Issue Spotting

Often, when people are involved in an interpersonal dispute, there is so much tension that the dispute escalates unnecessarily simply because each side has distorted perceptions about what the other party thinks, wants, expects, or believes. The TPI (Third-Party Intervener) can assist the disputing parties in identifying the issues or matters most relevant to the dispute. Additionally, the mediator can help each side better understand what the other side is thinking or feeling.

Consider that disputes have both manifest issues and underlying issues. For disputants, identifying their own underlying issues may be difficult. The TPI can use their skills to help draw out those underlying concerns. Knowing the underlying issues will help the disputants address the dispute more completely. If these issues are identified in the dispute resolution process, then the third party has helped the disputing parties clearly see what is being argued. When the parties have a clear understanding of the issues, they are more likely to resolve the dispute effectively.

2. Manage and Facilitate

Many times, two people or sides in an interpersonal dispute need structure to help them resolve their conflict. This is when a TPI is most needed. For example, because the parties are arguing, neither may reach out to the other to say, "Let's settle this argument." So, who brings these parties together to talk about their differences? The TPI is the best person to do so.

The mediator can coordinate bringing the parties together so that they can manage and oversee the dispute resolution process themselves. Facilitation best describes the function of the TPI when they manage a dispute.

By managing the dispute, the TPI keeps the process goal-directed. In other words, the mediator helps maintain focus on the matters that must be addressed rather than allowing the discussion to drift into irrelevant areas. The TPI uses a roadmap—a systematic process—to keep the resolution civil and effective. In doing so, the TPI also applies dispute resolution skills to keep the parties from shouting or behaving disruptively. The mediator facilitates the process, meaning they guide the parties in taking the steps necessary to resolve the matter they are disputing.

3. Education of the Disputants

Disputants may need to learn from TPIs that disputes are normal—everyone experiences them, and they are an integral part of life. Such an explanation may help disputants realize they are not deviant or abnormal for having a conflict. Sometimes disputants are unaware of the alternatives available to resolve their issues. The TPI can inform them of these options and advise which methods might be most or least appropriate for their particular dispute.

In some cases, the disputants may be unaware of laws, policies, or rules that impact the matter they are arguing about. The TPI can educate them about such influencing factors. Additionally, when in a dispute, people often have positions (what they want) and interests (why they want it—reasons like X, Y, and Z). The TPI can help disputants understand the difference between positions and interests. The mediator may explain that, in many cases, efforts to resolve a dispute should focus more on the underlying interests rather than on fixed positions.

4. Brainstorming Assistance

Sometimes the parties in dispute cannot clearly see how the conflict might be resolved. The TPI can assist in developing possible resolutions. Alternatives that may not be immediately obvious to the disputants could be evident to the TPI, who can help the parties explore new and constructive solutions.

5. Help Disputants to Save Face

"Face-saving reflects a person's need to reconcile the stand he takes in a negotiation or an agreement with his principles and with his past words and deeds" (Fisher and Ury, 1983, p. 29).

Sometimes people in dispute are adamant or determined to maintain a particular position (e.g., "I want the book returned, and I'll take nothing less—I never go back on my word"). When someone makes absolute statements, they are often unwilling to walk them back. The TPI can help in these situations by using dispute resolution skills to guide the disputant toward relaxing their position in a way that does not make them feel they have lost face.

6. Keep the Resolution Process Fair and Balanced

The TPI is needed to ensure that all disputants or parties have equal opportunity to participate in the resolution process. This helps ensure that agreements are not coerced by one party over another. When the TPI is the one making the final decision or resolution, as in arbitration, the mediator does so in an objective and impartial manner.

Chapter 16

The Negotiation Process

Negotiation is at the heart of all settlement and is included as one of the dispute resolution procedures facilitated by one or more third-party neutrals. When there is a successful negotiation, the dispute is resolved.

Negotiation is composed of various stages:

- Preparation and planning
- Ice breaking
- Agenda control
- Information bargaining
- Proposals, offers, demands
- Persuasions and justifications
- Concessions and reformulations
- Crisis: resolution or deadlock
- Closing
- Memorialization

Negotiation Theory

Term Theory: Refers to the underlying method of how the procedure or process of negotiation works.

Style Theory: An individual matter of choice that the negotiator makes.

Strategy Theory: A specific set of negotiating behaviors.

Two Primary Theories:

There is a dichotomy of negotiation as either distributive or integrative.

Distributive: There is a fixed pie with limited resources to be distributed. More for one necessarily means less for the other. This has also been described as a zero-sum game. Where there is a fixed quantity of resources, one person's gain is necessarily the other's loss.

Distributive Pie

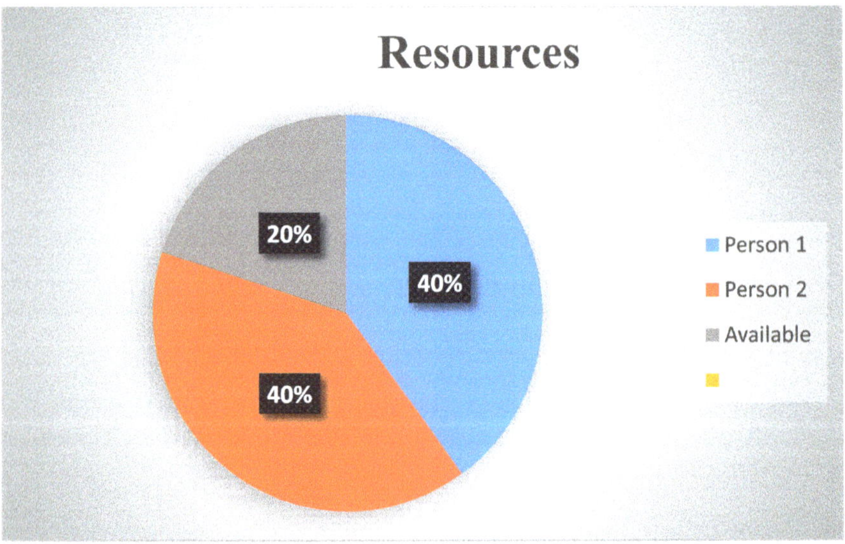

Integrative: This type of negotiation involves the exploration of several options, many of which are not in direct conflict with one another. An expanded pie exists, providing an opportunity for mutual gain. The interests of the parties are not necessarily in direct conflict, and therefore, there is no inherent inverse level of satisfaction in the process. There is room for creativity, and a collaborative problem-solving approach is usually observed in this type of negotiation.

Integrative Pie

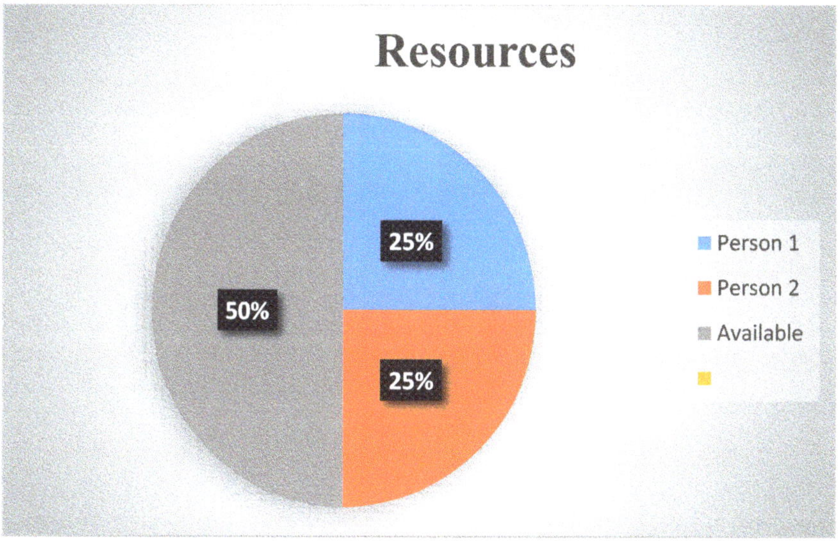

Positional Negotiation: The parties align themselves with a position and spend effort defending it against attack. They do not focus on what they really want. Instead, they remain stuck on their position or the cause and justification for the positions they take.

The specific styles identified with positional bargaining are hard and soft:

Hard: Negotiators are adversarial and confrontational. **Soft:** Friendly and cooperative. Soft negotiators often yield and concede to avoid confrontation.

Principled Negotiators: These negotiators attempt to identify underlying interests and generate several alternatives for settlement. The principled negotiator looks for possible solutions that might satisfy everyone's interests, with the objective being a final resolution with which everyone is satisfied.

Interest-Based Negotiators: These negotiators look to the underlying interests of the parties and use essentially the same approach taken in principled negotiation.

Rights-Based Negotiators: These negotiators look to the entitlement of rights between the parties to determine a solution based on those rights, similar to positional negotiation.

(Kovach, 2004, pp. 193–200)

Chapter 17

Co-Mediation

Co-mediation does not mean that one mediator is in charge and the other is subordinate. You are equal unless directed otherwise, such as when a new mediator is in training.

Very seldom, if ever, is there a team of more than two mediators. Only in extreme circumstances—such as a large group of disputants—are more than two mediators used simultaneously.

People are human, and disputes are a normal part of life. Some people will work well together, while others will not. In other words, some co-mediation teams may need to be re-arranged from time to time.

Below are tasks for mediators when practicing co-mediation. Since there are two mediators, make sure to do the following **before** the mediation begins:

1. Discuss the parts and roles that each of you will play. Make sure to agree on balancing your participation, or agree that one person will take the lead.
2. Discuss how you can interrupt each other in a way that is not disruptive or awkward.

In this regard, decide if there is a signal you want to use, either verbal or nonverbal, to indicate that you would like to meet privately in a mediator's meeting.

You must do your best to avoid doing anything that could cause embarrassment to your co-mediator or undermine the process by showing that you are not working as a team.

3. Discuss with each other how you will handle an impasse (that is, when the parties cannot agree to a resolution).
4. After the mediation, it may be helpful to discuss and debrief.

Chapter 18

Closure and Follow-Up

In addition to the agreement, a formal or symbolic activity that signifies the termination of the conflict should occur:

- Handshake
- Exchanging the agreement
- Meal
- A toast
- Any significant exchange, depending on the culture and type of mediation. The mediator should use discretion appropriate to the participants, issues, culture, and situation.

Closure is particularly important in cases where there has been a reconciliation between parties. The expression of apology and the extension of forgiveness may be important in certain cases, but the mediator should not compel the parties to do so. The process should allow such behavior if the parties wish for it to happen

(Kovach, 2004, p. 387).

Concluding the Mediation

Rarely do mediations continue indefinitely until an agreement is reached. Where the time is not definite, reaching the agreement is the primary indication that the process is ending (Kovach, 2004, p. 390).

Closure with Formal Mediated Agreement

Most mediated agreements result in a written document. Some closing remarks and rituals may occur during the time the mediator drafts the agreement. In other instances, remarks or symbolic activities take place after the agreement is signed.

The mediator must always remember that—before, during, and after the mediation—they are a neutral third party. After an agreement is reached, written, signed, and distributed, the mediator should still maintain neutrality.

In closing, the mediator should ensure that the following items are addressed and clearly provided for:

1. The parties have exchanged any necessary information such as addresses and telephone numbers.
2. Everyone has a copy of the agreement.
3. Any follow-up between the parties or the mediator is clear and specific.
4. All dates, times, and places are clarified, preferably in writing (Kovach, 2004, p. 391).

Closure Without Formal Agreement

If no agreement is reached, the mediator need not explain to the parties in detail why the mediation is being terminated. The mediator should explain only that it has reached an impasse and should do so in a positive manner.

Follow-up is often appropriate. Nonetheless, it is recognized that in some instances, continued negotiation would be futile and should not be recommended.

Where the mediation was volatile and face-to-face confrontation could be explosive, the mediator should take care to ensure that the parties leave at different times.

The rule of thumb when considering whether to reschedule the mediation is to ask: Can something tangible be achieved by meeting again? (Kovach, 2004, pp. 391–392)

Post-Mediation Follow-Up

In instances where the mediation terminates without an agreement, some mediators continue negotiations with both sides by telephone in an effort to achieve a settlement. The mediator should not continually harass the parties in the hope that they will be motivated to settle.

In many cases, follow-up by the mediator is typically appreciated by the parties and is viewed as evidence of the mediator's sincere commitment to the process (Kovach, 2004, p. 392).

Chapter 19

Restorative Justice

How Can We Use Restorative Practices?

Tier 3 (Top): Restoring Relationships – Intensive (1–5%)

Tier 2 (Middle): Resolving Conflict – Targeted (as required)

Tier 1 (Bottom): Preventing Conflict and Harm – Universal (100%)

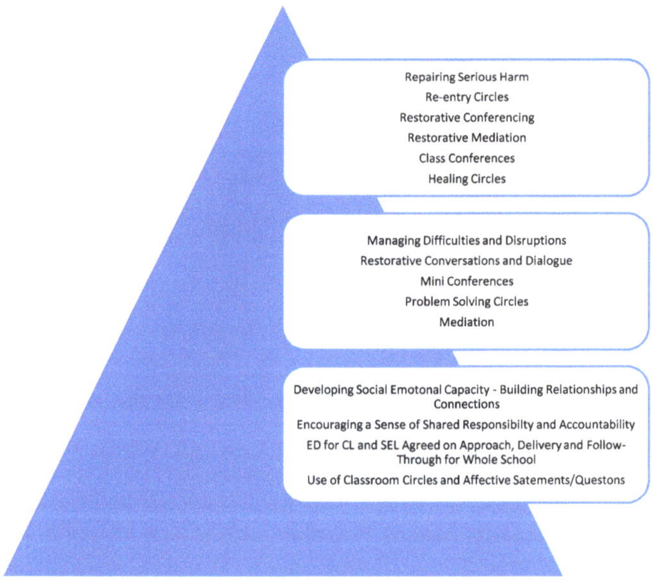

Restorative Justice – crc-global.org

What Is Restorative Justice

Collins (2015) provides an answer to what restorative justice is through a twelve-part question-and-answer explanation.

1. **What is restorative justice?**

   Restorative justice gives victims the chance to meet or communicate with their offender to explain the real impact of the crime. It empowers victims by giving them a voice. It also holds offenders accountable for what they have done and helps them take responsibility and make amends. Restorative justice often involves a conference where a victim meets their offender face to face. Sometimes, when a face-to-face meeting is not the best way forward, the victim and offender will communicate via letters, recorded interviews, or video.

2. **Why would I take part?**

   Many victims feel that the criminal justice system does not give them a chance to get involved. Restorative justice puts victims at the heart of the justice process. It gives you a chance to ask the offender any questions you may have and to say what you need to about the impact of the crime. Government research shows that 85% of victims who take part in restorative justice find the process helpful. For many victims, meeting the person who has harmed them can be a huge step in moving forward and recovering from the crime. Restorative justicc also helps reduce crime. Research shows it reduces reoffending by 14%.

3. **How will I know what to do?**

   The restorative justice process is led by a facilitator who supports and prepares the people taking part and ensures the process is safe. They will walk you through it, answer any questions, and explain what will happen at each stage. This is your opportunity to explore what will work best for you, and it is entirely your decision whether to proceed. You can drop out at any time.

4. **When can restorative justice take place?**

   Restorative justice can take place at any point in the criminal justice process. For minor offenses, the police may deal with the issue without going to court, and restorative justice can be part of that. If the case does go to court and the offender pleads guilty, a judge or magistrate may delay sentencing so restorative justice can happen. More commonly, however, sentencing proceeds, and restorative justice becomes part of a community or suspended sentence. If the offender is sent to prison, restorative justice can occur while they are incarcerated or after their release. The important thing is that it can happen at any stage, but it must be the right time for you.

5. **Which offenses can restorative justice be used for?**

   Restorative justice can potentially be used for any type of crime. It can help victims of low-level offenses as well as people affected by the most serious crimes. Some offenses—

such as sexual offenses, hate crimes, and domestic violence—present particular challenges for the restorative process. However, restorative justice can still support victims of these offenses. It is essential that these cases are handled by senior practitioners with the relevant experience and skills.

6. **Is restorative justice safe?**

   Yes. Facilitators are trained to assess risks and ensure the process is safe for everyone involved. They will not allow a conference to go ahead unless they are confident it can be done safely. You will never be left alone with the offender, and the facilitator will support you throughout the process.

7. **Where would a meeting take place?**

   A restorative justice meeting takes place in a safe and neutral venue. It could be a police station, a probation office, or a community center. If the offender is in prison, the meeting may be held in an appropriate room inside the facility. The facilitator will discuss the location with you so you know what to expect. You may also have input on how the room is arranged, including where everyone sits.

8. **Can I have a friend or family member with me?**

   Yes. Some people prefer to attend on their own, but others bring a friend or family member for support. This will be discussed and agreed upon in advance with the facilitator so the supporter is fully prepared. Even if you choose to attend alone, the facilitator will always be present, and you will never be left alone with the offender.

9. **Do I have to meet the offender face to face?**

   No. If a face-to-face meeting is not the best option, the facilitator may arrange communication through letters, recorded interviews, or video. Whether you meet the offender in person is entirely up to you. However, research has shown that face-to-face meetings are often the most satisfying form of restorative justice for victims.

10. **Can I stop the process at any time?**

    Yes. Restorative justice is entirely voluntary. You can stop at any point, including on the day of the conference or even during the meeting itself. The facilitator will support you and help avoid surprises, but the final decision is always yours.

11. **Do I need to forgive my offender to take part?**

    No. Forgiveness is not a requirement. During preparation, the facilitator will ensure that you are emotionally ready to meet the offender, but they will not stop you from participating if you have strong negative feelings. Anger is a natural response, and expressing it can be an important part of the process.

12. **How can I find out more?**

To learn more about restorative justice, visit the Restorative Justice Council's website at www.restorativejustice.org.uk. It includes details on how to access restorative justice in your area (p. 4, 5).

Ethical Standards of Professional Responsibility

SPIDR Ethics Committee

These standards were adopted by SPIDR on June 2, 1986. They are currently under review by the ACR Standards Committee for the Association for Conflict Resolution.

Introduction

The Society of Professionals in Dispute Resolution (SPIDR) was established in 1972 to promote the peaceful resolution of disputes. Members of the Society believe that resolving disputes through negotiation, mediation, arbitration, and other neutral interventions can benefit disputing parties and society as a whole.

In 1983, the SPIDR Board of Directors charged the Ethics Committee with developing ethical standards of professional responsibility. The committee was composed of representatives from all sectors and disciplines within SPIDR. This document, adopted by the Board on June 2, 1986, is the result of that effort.

The purpose of this document is to promote ethical conduct and a high level of competency among SPIDR members and associates. It emphasizes honesty, integrity, impartiality, and the exercise of sound judgment in dispute resolution efforts. It is also intended to help:

1. Define the profession of dispute resolution
2. Educate the public
3. Inform users of dispute resolution services

Application of Standards

Adherence to these ethical standards by SPIDR Members and Associates is fundamental to professional responsibility. SPIDR Members and Associates commit themselves to be guided in their professional conduct by these standards. The SPIDR Board of Directors or its designee is available to advise Members and Associates on the interpretation of these standards. Other neutral practitioners and organizations are welcome to follow these standards.

Scope

It is recognized that SPIDR Members and Associates resolve disputes in various sectors within the disciplines of dispute resolution and may have their own codes of professional conduct. These standards have been developed as general guidelines of practice for the neutral disciplines represented in SPIDR membership. Ethical considerations relevant to some, but not all, of these disciplines are not covered by these standards.

General Responsibilities

Neutrals have a duty to the parties, to the profession, and to themselves. They should be honest and unbiased, act in good faith, be diligent, and not seek to advance their own interests at the expense of the parties.

Neutrals must act fairly in dealing with the parties, have no personal interest in the terms of the settlement, show no bias toward individuals or institutions involved in the dispute, be reasonably available as requested by the parties, and ensure that the parties are informed of the process in which they are involved.

1. **Impartiality**

   The neutral must maintain impartiality toward all parties. Impartiality means freedom from favoritism or bias, either by word or action, and a commitment to serve all parties equally rather than favoring a single party.

2. **Informed Consent**

   The neutral has an obligation to ensure that all parties understand the nature of the process, the procedures involved, the neutral's role, and the relationship between the neutral and the parties.

3. **Confidentiality**

   Maintaining confidentiality is critical to the dispute resolution process. It encourages candor, facilitates full exploration of issues, and enhances a neutral's acceptability. Some types of cases may not be protected by confidentiality, and in such instances, the neutral must inform the parties, at an appropriate time in the process, that confidentiality may not be guaranteed. Except in those instances, the neutral must resist attempts to reveal any information outside the process. The neutral's commitment to confidentiality must be upheld at all times.

4. **Conflict of Interest**

   The neutral must refrain from entering into or continuing in any dispute if participation would present a clear conflict of interest or any circumstance that could reasonably raise questions about impartiality. The duty to disclose is ongoing throughout the process.

5. **Promptness**

   The neutral shall make every reasonable effort to expedite the process.

6. **The Settlement and Its Consequences**

   The dispute resolution process belongs to the parties. The neutral has no vested interest in the terms of the settlement but must ensure that the integrity of the process is not compromised by the outcome. The neutral has a responsibility to help the parties consider the terms of the settlement. If the neutral is concerned about the consequences of an agreement, and the needs of the parties warrant it, they must inform the parties of that concern. In doing so, the neutral may choose to educate the parties, refer one or more parties for specialized advice, or withdraw from the case. However, the neutral must not violate Section 3, Confidentiality.

Unrepresented Interests

The neutral must consider circumstances in which certain interests are not represented in the process. Where appropriate, the neutral has an obligation to ensure that such interests are considered by the principal parties.

Use of Multiple Procedures

The use of more than one dispute resolution procedure by the same neutral carries additional responsibilities. If multiple procedures are initially contemplated, the neutral must inform the parties of the nature of each procedure and the consequences of sharing information that may later influence decision-making. If a transition to another procedure is proposed after the process has begun, the neutral must explain the implications and offer the parties an opportunity to choose another neutral. The neutral must clearly notify all parties when transitioning between processes.

Background and Qualifications

A neutral should accept responsibility only in cases where they possess sufficient knowledge of the process and subject matter. Neutrals are responsible for maintaining and improving their professional skills.

Disclosure of Fees

At the beginning of the process, the neutral must clearly explain the basis of compensation, including all fees and charges.

Support of the Profession

Experienced neutrals should contribute to the development of new practitioners and educate the public about the value and use of neutral dispute resolution methods. They are encouraged to provide pro bono services where appropriate.

Responsibilities of Neutrals Working on the Same Case

When more than one neutral is involved in a case, each must inform the others of their participation. Neutrals working together must maintain open, respectful, and professional relationships with one another.

Advertising and Solicitation

Neutrals must be mindful that certain forms of advertising and solicitation are inappropriate or impermissible, especially in disciplines such as labor arbitration. Advertising must honestly represent the services offered. Claims of specific results or promises suggesting favoritism are not allowed. Neutrals must not give or receive commissions, rebates, or similar payments for client referrals.

References

1. Arsovska, J., & Verduyn, P. (2008). Globalization, conduct norms and 'culture conflict': Perceptions of violence and crime in an ethnic Albanian context. *The British Journal of Criminology, 48*(2), 226–246. Retrieved from https://doi.org/10.1093/bjc/azm068
2. Bretscher, J. P., & Haugk, K. C. (2023). *The gift of empathy: Helping others feel valued, cared for, and understood.* St. Louis, MO: Stephen Ministry.
3. Collins, J. (2015). *What is restorative justice*. Center for Restorative Justice and Peacemaking | UMN Duluth. Retrieved from https://rjp.d.umn.edu
4. Cooper, C. (1999). *Mediation and arbitration by patrol police officers*. Lanham, MD: University Press.
5. Creative Response to Conflict. (2021). Retrieved from https://crc-global.org
6. Cultural Conflict. (n.d.). Retrieved from https://study.com
7. Eleveld, M. (2003). *The spoken word revolution (slam, hip hop & the poetry of a new generation)*. Naperville, IL: Sourcebooks, Inc.
8. Exchange Theory. (n.d.). Retrieved from https://www.encyclopedia.com

9. Fisher, R., & Ury, W. (1983). *Getting to yes: Negotiating agreement without giving in*. New York, NY: Penguin Books USA, Inc.
10. Goffman, E. (1959). *The presentation of self in everyday life*. New York, NY: Doubleday.
11. Hass, A. Y., Moloney, C., & Chambliss, W. J. (2017). *Criminology: Connecting theory, research, and practice* (2nd ed.). New York, NY: Routledge.
12. Kovach, K. (2004). *Mediation: Principles and practice* (3rd ed.). St. Paul, MN: West Publishing Co.
13. Kriesberg, L. (2009). *The Sage handbook of conflict resolution*. Thousand Oaks, CA: Sage.
14. Molinaro, P. J. (2024). *The history of mediation*. Retrieved from https://www.mdjddisputeresolution.com
15. Molm, L. D., Takahashi, N., & Peterson, G. (2000). Risk and trust in social exchange: An experimental test of a classical proposition. *American Journal of Sociology, 105*(5), 1396–1427.
16. Nickerson, C. (2021, September). *Anomie*. Simply Psychology Research. Retrieved from https://www.simplypsychology.org/anomie.html
17. Paternoster, R., Jaynes, C. M., & Wilson, T. (2017). Rational choice theory, and interest in the "fortune of others." *Journal of Research in Crime and Delinquency, 54*(6), 847–868.

18. Picard, C. A. (1998). *Mediating interpersonal and small group conflict*. Ottawa, CA: The Golden Dog Press.
19. Randolph, P. (2016). *The psychology of conflict: Mediating in a diverse world*. New York, NY: Bloomsbury Publishing Plc.
20. Rosenberg, M. B. (2015). *Nonviolent communication: A language of life* (3rd ed.). Encinitas, CA: Puddle Dancer Press.
21. Schmalleger, F. (2006). *Criminology today: An integrative introduction* (4th ed.). Saddle River, NJ: Pearson Prentice Hall.
22. Siegel, L., & Worrall, J. L. (2018). *Introduction to criminal justice* (16th ed.). Boston, MA: Cengage Learning.
23. Seltzer, L. F. (2014, April). *6 virtues and 6 vices of venting*. Retrieved from https://www.psychologytoday.com
24. Slaikeu, K. A. (1996). *When push comes to shove: A practical guide to mediating disputes*. San Francisco, CA: Jossey-Bass Inc.
25. Sockolov, M. (2018). *Practicing mindfulness: 75 essential meditations to reduce stress, improve mental health, and find peace in the everyday*. Emeryville, CA: Althea Press.
26. SPIDR Ethics Committee. (1986). Retrieved from https://www.cabq.gov/legal/adr/land-use-facilitation/facilitator-tool-box/ethical-standards

27. Spotted Eagle, F. (2000). *Many paths, many spirits: Liberation from oppression, peacekeeping, leadership skillbuilding, organizational development*. Mission, SD: Spotted Eagle & Associates.

28. Vito, G. F., & Maahs, J. R. (2017). *Criminology: Theory, research, and policy* (4th ed.). Burlington, MA: Jones & Bartlett Learning.

Yluiia, S. (2020). The origins and the development of mediation. *European Proceedings of the Social and Behavioural Sciences, 10*(5), 2453–2458.

www.ingramcontent.com/pod-product-compliance
Lightning Source LLC
Chambersburg PA
CBHW041259210926
51847CB00009B/78
9781968966355